942.05

The making of the United Kingdom

CHARLES MALTMAN *and* IAN DAWSON

Contents

D1422005

Oxford University Press

Oxford University Press,
Great Clarendon Street,
Oxford OX2 6DP

*Oxford New York Athens
Auckland Bangkok Bogota
Bombay Buenos Aires Calcutta
Cape Town Dar es Salaam Delhi
Florence Hong Kong Istanbul
Karachi Kuala Lumpur Madras
Madrid Melbourne Mexico City
Nairobi Paris Singapore Taipei
Tokyo Toronto*

and associated companies in
Berlin Ibadan

Typeset by MS Filmsetting
Limited, Frome, Somerset
Printed in Italy

✳ Preface

Like the other books in this series, *The making
of the United Kingdom* is structured as an
investigation. It focusses on the central
question: 'Which changes were most important
between 1500 and 1750?', a question that can be
explored and answered by pupils at a variety of
levels, depending upon their ability. Having
established the question, the first chapter
invites pupils to put forward an initial
hypothesis, using their existing ideas,
assumptions or prejudices. Each succeeding
chapter then examines a single theme and offers
the chance for pupils to revise their initial
hypothesis. The initial answers from groups or
individuals should be recorded (in pupils' books
or as a wall-display) and then developed as
pupils explore each question in more detail. As
a conclusion, a comparison between the initial
answers and the final conclusions should boost
pupils' confidence by helping them appreciate
how much they have learned about life in
Britain between 1500 and 1750.

The structure of the book is thematic and
teachers may choose to vary the order in which
topics are studied. There are several
opportunities to speed progress by dividing
work up amongst different groups of students
in the class. For example, in chapter three each
group could examine one of the turning-points
in the power of the monarchy so that the class
as a whole could complete the grid on page 23
in one lesson. In chapter six half the class could
study Ireland, the other half Scotland before
comparing conclusions using the chart on page
57. In chapter seven groups could examine
British relations with different countries,
France, Spain or the Netherlands before again
producing an overall comparison.

The central question about change was not
chosen haphazardly. The focus on change,
continuity and causation means that teachers
can develop pupils' understanding of the Key
Elements without resorting to 'add-on'
exercises.

Charles Maltman   Ian Dawson

✳ Notes to teachers

Exercises offering opportunities for developing
pupils' understanding of concepts and skills
required in the Key Elements are signposted
as follows. Questions at the end of each
chapter open up opportunities for explicit
discussion of the concepts that lie behind the
Key Elements. Such explicit discussion is vital
for the development of pupils' understanding.

CHANGE AND MORE CHANGE

A fifteenth century picture of Earl Rivers presenting a printed book to Edward IV. The man kneeling on the left may be Caxton.

A page from one of Caxton's early books. The print was deliberately made to look like handwriting so that people would not be shocked by the change from handwriting to printing. This page is from Chaucer's *Canterbury Tales*.

Sometime in 1477 William Caxton delivered an extraordinary book to Anthony, Earl Rivers. It was very expensive and very beautiful but these were not the reasons why it was extraordinary. It was so remarkable because it was printed, not handwritten. It was the first book to be printed in Britain. In the next few years Caxton printed many more books, mostly religious books or histories but also books on hunting, chess and other pastimes.

Many people in England could read, perhaps thirty per cent overall, and more in London and other large towns. The scriveners, the people who copied books by hand, could not keep up with the demand for books. So there was a need for a new method of making books. Caxton brought the idea of printing from the Netherlands, where he had lived and worked as a merchant. Printing presses were working all over Europe because of this great demand.

Not everyone supported this change. The scriveners feared they would be completely out of work because of printing. However, printing did develop and in the next two hundred years this new technology helped to change many aspects of life in Britain. Caxton and the other early printers would have been surprised by these changes. After all, they had tried to make their books look as much like handwritten books as possible so that people would feel comfortable with the new technology. Printing was not meant to revolutionise anything – but it did.

Can you suggest how the development of printing might affect religion, the power of the monarch, education or any other aspect of life in Britain?

✳ Famous people and events: 1500–1750

Source A

Fountains Abbey in Yorkshire
All the abbeys and monasteries were closed by Henry VIII after he left the Roman Catholic Church and started the Church of England.

Source B

Source C

Source D

The introduction of printing was one of the most important developments in the whole of British history. Many other important or exciting events also took place between 1500 and 1750, the years you are going to investigate in this book. You can see some of these events on these pages. You may be able to recognise some of them already. By answering the questions below you will start to build up your knowledge of what happened in Britain at that time.

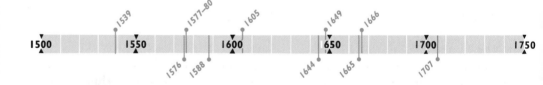

FAMOUS PEOPLE AND EVENTS

1 You can see the pictures of five people on these pages. Who is shown in Sources B, C, D, M and N?

2 The timeline gives you the dates of ten events mentioned or shown on these pages. Copy the timeline and put the name of the correct event next to each date.

3 Which events are connected with the people on these pages?

4 There were other important changes in British life (between 1500 and 1750) besides the development of printing. Try to find important changes connected with:

a religion

b the power of the monarch

c England's links with other countries.

Source E

Lieutenant General Cromwell had with much gallantry charged through and routed two Brigades of Horse in the enemy's right wing, who were the bravest men Prince Rupert had. Our Horse and Foot put the rest of the enemy's right wing to flight, forcing them from their cannon and ammunition. Our left wing charged every group remaining in the field, until all were fully routed and put to flight. Our men pursued the enemy about three miles until they came near to York.

(An account of the Battle of Marston Moor, written in the seventeenth century)

Source F

Drake captured Don Pedro of Valdez, Admiral of fourteen vessels and had him and ten other nobles brought onto his own ship. He gave them a banquet and treated them very handsomely. There is news that eighteen ships of the Spanish Armada were sunk by gunfire and eight taken and brought to England. The rest of the Spanish Armada had fled.

(From a newsletter written by a German merchant)

Source G

Thomas Percy hired a house at Westminster, near the Parliament House, and there we began to make our mine. The five who entered into this work were Thomas Percy, Robert Catesby, Thomas Winter, John Wright and myself. We brought into the House twenty barrels of powder.

(From the confession of Guy Fawkes)

Source H

There came unto us a number of boats, and in one of them the king's brother, accompanied with 40 or 50 men, very handsome and goodly people, and in their behaviour as mannerly and civil as any of Europe. His name was Granganimeo, and the king is called Wingina; the country Wingandacoa and now after Her Majesty, Virginia. When we came to the shore to him, with our weapons, he never moved from his place nor mistrusted any harm to be offered from us.

(An account of the first English settlements in Virginia, America, written by Master Arthur Barlowe, one of the captains, and sent to Sir Walter Raleigh who organised the voyage)

Source I

Her Majesty came this day to the House of Lords and was pleased to give the Royal Assent to 'An Act for a Union of the Two Kingdoms of England and Scotland'. After which Her Majesty made a most gracious speech:

'My Lords and Gentlemen, It is with the greatest satisfaction that I have given my assent to a Bill for Uniting England and Scotland into one Kingdom. I consider this Union as a matter of the greatest importance to the wealth, strength and safety of the whole Island....'

(The London Gazette)

Source J

On the day of his execution I stood amongst the crowd in the street before Whitehall gate where the scaffold was erected, and saw what was done, but was not so near as to hear anything. The blow I saw given, at the instant whereof, I remember well, there was such a groan by the thousands then present as I never heard before and desire I may never hear again.

(Diary of Philip Henry, who witnessed the execution of King Charles I)

Source K

I walked to the Tower ... and there I did see the houses at that end of the bridge all on fire and an infinite great fire on this and the other side and end of the bridge ... The Lieutenant of the Tower tells me that it began this morning in the King's baker's house in Pudding Lane.

(Samuel Pepys, Diary)

Source L

7 June: The hottest day that ever I felt in my life ... I did in Drury Lane see two or three houses marked with a red cross upon the doors and 'Lord, have mercy on us' writ there.

20 July: There died 1,089 of the plague this week.

31 August: In the city died this week 7,496 and of them 6,102 of the plague.

20 September: What a sad time it is to see no boats upon the river; and grass grows all up and down White Hall court.

(Samuel Pepys, Diary)

Source M

Source N

Source O

The Golden Hind
The ship in which Francis Drake sailed around the world

❋ Life in Britain: 1066–1750

You have already investigated life in Britain in the Middle Ages, between 1066 and 1500. Many things did not change much during those five hundred years but sometimes changes came quickly. The population fell rapidly after the Black Death arrived in 1348. Then in the fifteenth century many people became more prosperous. They had better housing and clothing, higher wages and more food and, as you read on page 3, they were better educated. Therefore life was changing more quickly in the 1400s, at the end of the Middle Ages.

English Population 1100–1500

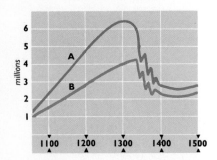

Historians are unsure about the exact number of people in Britain in the Middle Ages. However, we do know that the total rose and then fell after the Black Death.

Line A shows the highest number estimated by historians. Line B shows the lowest number.

England and Britain
England took control of Wales and a small part of Ireland. Scotland had fought hard to keep her independence.

Daily life
Living standards gradually improved after 1000 but then fell 1250–1350. People became much richer in the 1400s. Instead of being villeins tied to the land, most people became free after the Black Death and Peasants' Revolt.

Europe and the world
England lost her empire in France after a long series of wars. There were few other wars. Most trade was with other countries in Western Europe.

King and Parliament
The king was always very powerful. He had to ask Parliament for taxes but Parliament only met when the king needed it.

Changes and continuities 1066–1500

Religion
Religion stayed very important for everyone. All English people belonged to the Roman Catholic Church, headed by the Pope.

England and Britain
England and Scotland were united by James VI and I in 1603 and the Act of Union in 1707. English control over Ireland increased but they were divided by religion.

Daily life
The population steadily increased. Many people became wealthier but some lost work. Towns grew larger. Housing, clothing and diet all improved and became more varied. Many schools were started.

Europe and the world
England built up a new empire, mostly in America. There was trade with countries all over the world but also wars with Spain, France and the Dutch.

Monarch and Parliament
Parliament became much more powerful after the Civil War and the Revolution of 1688. The monarch had to call Parliament regularly. By 1750 the monarch had a Prime Minister who needed the support of both them and Parliament.

Changes and continuities 1500–1750

Religion
The Church of England was started in the 1530s. Disagreements between Protestants and Catholics caused wars and rebellions.

Between 1500 and 1750 some things still stayed the same. We call these 'continuities'. For example, people still travelled on foot, on horseback or in carriages pulled by horses, just as they had done for centuries. However, there were also some very important changes and some of them were rapid and dramatic. The charts on these pages summarise these continuities and changes. See if you can use this information (and any other evidence you have) to check whether each of the following statements are correct:

● There were more continuities than changes in the Middle Ages.
● There were some important changes in the Middle Ages.
● There was more change between 1500–1750 than 1066–1500.
● There were continuities as well as changes between 1500 and 1750.

English Population 1500–1750

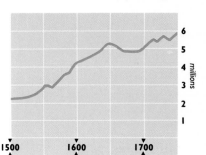

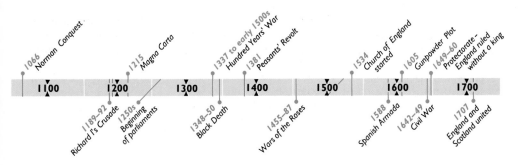

Stages of investigation

In this book you will be investigating the changes in Britain between 1500 and 1750. These are the stages of your investigation.

Stage 1
Start with a question

Which of these changes was the most important?

Stage 2
Suggest an answer even if you aren't sure

changes in daily life were probably the most important

Stage 3
Investigate what happened in the past

That was more important than I thought

Stage 4
Revise your first answer or hypothesis

That first answer wasn't bad but this is better...

✳ Investigating Britain: 1500–1750

This book will help you to investigate life in Britain between 1500 and 1750. You will be studying five topics – religion, everyday life, the power of the monarch, England's power in Britain, and Britain's involvement abroad. Your task will be to answer this question.

⧉ *Which were the most important changes for the people of Britain?*

The chart below lists the five topics for investigation. Draw your own copy of this chart and fill in the first column. If you think a change was very important give it 9 or 10 out of 10. If you think it was not so important give it a lower number. This will show your first ideas or hypotheses about which were the most important changes.

Then, as you work through the evidence in this book, you can complete the other columns. At the end of each chapter you will be able to complete column 5 and compare your conclusions with your first ideas and see how your answers have developed.

Each chapter will also investigate why things changed but also why others stayed the same in Britain between 1500 and 1750. Look at the list of reasons on the left.

● Which reasons do you think were the most important?
● Explain why you chose those reasons.

At the end of each chapter look at your answers again. Then you will be able to add to it or change it, depending on the evidence you find.

Reasons for change
● Ideas spread more quickly because of printing.
● The population gradually increased.
● Powerful or clever people wanted changes.
● Many people became richer and better educated.

Reasons for continuity
● People do not like change because it can be confusing.
● Many people were still poor and illiterate.
● Transport did not become quicker.

	1 *First answer* Was it an important change? (1–10)	2 Were many people affected by the changes?	3 Were the effects of the changes long-lasting?	4 Were the changes rapid or slow?	5 *Revised answer* Was it an important change? (1–10)	6 Did these changes help to unite Britain?	7 Do these changes still affect us today?
Religion							
Everyday life							
The power of the monarch							
England's power in Britain							
British involvement abroad							

RELIGION AND THE PEOPLE

▦ Margaret Clitherow – a religious martyr

Everyone has heard of Guy Fawkes, an ordinary man from York who tried to do an extraordinary thing. He tried to blow up Parliament and the Protestant King James I so that the country would turn back to the Catholic religion. You probably have not heard of Margaret Clitherow, another ordinary person from York whose life was remarkable. Margaret also died for the Catholic religion.

Margaret was born in about 1556. She married John Clitherow in 1571, and they lived in the Shambles, a street you can still walk along today. John belonged to the Church of England, as the law said everyone must. Everyone had to attend church every week and non-attenders were fined or imprisoned. Catholics were regarded as potential traitors who might help a Spanish invasion to remove Queen Elizabeth from the throne.

In 1574 Margaret decided that she really believed in the Catholic faith. She put herself in danger by hiding Catholic priests (who were outlawed) and attending the Catholic Mass regularly. Margaret spent several periods in prison before she was arrested for the final time in July 1586.

The most serious charge was hiding priests. Margaret refused to plead guilty to something she did not think was a crime. But if she pleaded not guilty the judges would use her small children as witnesses to prove her guilt. Margaret did not want her children to blame themselves for her death so she refused to plead either guilty or not guilty, even though she knew that the penalty for refusing to plead was horrific.

When she did not plead, the judges had no choice but to condemn her to be crushed to death. Margaret is reported to have said, 'God be thanked, I am not worthy of so good a death as this.' On Good Friday, 1586, Margaret was taken from prison to her execution. She was placed on the ground with a sharp stone beneath her spine. A door was placed on top of her and weighted down until she was crushed to death. Her last words were, 'Jesu, Jesu, Jesu, have mercy on me!'

Margaret Clitherow was just one of many people who died for their religion in the 1500s and 1600s. This was a time of great changes in religion. In this chapter you will be investigating those changes and answering this question:

● *Were the religious changes important for the people?*

How does the story of Margaret Clitherow help you to begin your investigation?

Both Catholics and Protestants became martyrs – people who were executed because of their religious beliefs. In Mary Tudor's reign, two of the most famous Protestant martyrs were bishops Nicholas Ridley and Hugh Latimer. As the burning began, Latimer said 'Be of good comfort, Master Ridley, and play the man. We shall this day light such a candle, by God's grace, in England as I trust shall never be put out.'

⚞ Changes in religion

In the Middle Ages there was only one kind of Christian religion in Western Europe. All Western Christians were Roman Catholics. The leader of their Church was the Pope in Rome. The Pope, the bishops and the priests told people that if they believed in the true religion, they would go to heaven after they died. This would be their reward for believing in God and for the struggles and hardships of their lives. As most people had short, difficult lives they wanted to believe in their reward in heaven.

Therefore it was vital to believe in the right religion, otherwise you had no chance of going to heaven. People who did not believe in this true Christian religion were damned to suffer tortures in hell for ever. This meant that all other religions were completely wrong, but people in other religions could be saved if they changed their beliefs — by persuasion or by torture. If they would not change they were burned as heretics or unbelievers.

Heretics could not be allowed to live because their ideas were dangerous. If their ideas spread, more people would be in danger of going to hell instead of their after-life in heaven. They were also a danger because by refusing to accept the country's religion they were disobeying the monarch. Disobedience might encourage others to disobey the king or queen by refusing to pay taxes or obey the law.

Christian Europe was known as Christendom. Although wars between countries were common, kings sometimes worked together to fight for their religion on Crusades against people of other religions. Their enemies were Moslems in Spain and the Middle East or the people of Eastern Europe who were not Christians. Sometimes there were even Crusades in Europe against people whose ideas about Christianity were only slightly different from the beliefs of the Pope and the priests. Even these people were burned as heretics. Nobody was allowed to have different religious beliefs.

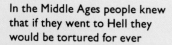

In the Middle Ages people knew that if they went to Hell they would be tortured for ever

The Reformation

In the sixteenth century there was a great change in religion when new kinds of Christianity developed. This reform, which is called the 'Reformation', began in Germany when people began to protest against the Roman Catholic Church. These protesters said that the Pope and the priests were not following the ideas or words of God and Jesus Christ closely enough. They said that the Church and its priests were too rich and that complicated services in Latin did not help the ordinary people to understand their religion.

These protesters, or Protestants, began their own kinds of Christian religion in different parts of Europe.

There were many Protestants in Germany and the Netherlands. England also left the Roman Catholic Church. Henry VIII began the Church of England and he became the head of the Church instead of the Pope. But that was only the beginning of change in England. You can see in the diagram below how the ideas of the Church of England later changed from reign to reign.

Changes in religion had many effects on the people of Britain. Many people, like Margaret Clitherow, wanted to stay Roman Catholic, but the law said they had to belong to the Church of England. People were still not allowed to choose their own religion.

Religious differences in Europe and England

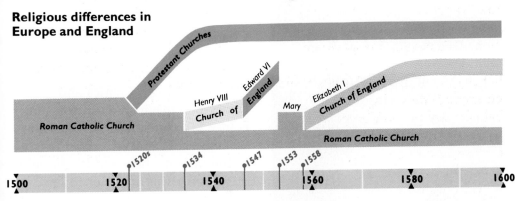

Protestant churches were plain. Their services were in the everyday language, not Latin. Ordinary people were allowed to read the Bible and priests were much less powerful. Altars were replaced by simple tables.

The Church of England changed its ideas from reign to reign. At first it did not move far from Catholic ideas but under Edward VI it became more Protestant. Mary returned England to Catholicism before Elizabeth changed the Church for the last time.

The Roman Catholic Church was led by the Pope. Bishops and priests were very powerful. Churches were richly decorated with statues and candles. The service of the Mass was in Latin. France and Spain remained strongly Catholic.

PEOPLE IN THE PAST: THE IMPORTANCE OF RELIGION

1 What ideas did people have about religion in the Middle Ages?
2 What are the differences between medieval Christianity and Christianity today?
3 How did religion change in the sixteenth century?
4 Why do you think everyone in England was forced to belong to the new Church instead of being allowed to choose their own religion?
5 Do you think that ideas about religion in the 1500s and 1600s were more like today's ideas or more like medieval ideas? Give reasons for your answer.

The beginning of religious change

How did the religious revolution begin in England? Why did Henry VIII start the Church of England? On these pages you can see four possible causes of this change. Read these causes and then answer the questions on page 13.

Henry VIII as a young man. He was a great athlete, always hunting and jousting, and he was also very intelligent.

Catherine of Aragon
Henry VIII's first wife.
She had been married for a short time to Henry's elder brother Arthur, who died in 1502. Catherine strongly believed in the Catholic faith and struggled bravely to stop the divorce from Henry. Her supporters quoted this verse from the Book of Deuteronomy in the Bible: 'When brethren dwell together, and one of them dieth without children, the wife of the deceased shall not marry to another, but his brother shall take her.'

Anne Boleyn
Henry's second wife.
She was a very intelligent woman and believed in the new Protestant ideas. Her supporters said that Henry should never have married Catherine because of this verse from Leviticus in the Bible: 'If a man shall take his brother's wife, it is an impurity. They shall be childless.'

Cause 1: Henry VIII and the succession

In 1529 Henry VIII had been married to Catherine of Aragon for twenty years. Henry thought it was vital to have a son to succeed him as king but they only had a daughter, Mary. Henry blamed Catherine for not having a son. At the same time, he had fallen in love with Anne Boleyn. Henry convinced himself that he should end his marriage to Catherine and marry Anne. He thought she would be certain to have a son!

As a Catholic, Henry asked the Pope to say that his marriage to Catherine was unlawful. Unfortunately, the Pope's lands had been conquered by the Emperor Charles V and the Pope had to follow Charles's instructions. Charles would not help Henry. A few years earlier, Charles and Henry had made an alliance against France but Henry had not kept the agreement. Charles was also Catherine's nephew and he thought the divorce was an insult to his aunt. The Pope did not give in to Henry.

Henry tried to put pressure on the Pope, including stopping taxes that were paid in England to the Pope. However, he eventually realised that the Pope would not agree. Then Anne Boleyn became pregnant. Henry needed to act quickly so that her baby would be legitimate. Guided by Thomas Cromwell, Henry started the Church of England with himself as its head and appointed Thomas Cranmer as Archbishop of Canterbury. Cranmer declared that the marriage to Catherine was over and then married Henry to Anne. A few months later their child was born – a daughter, called Elizabeth.

Cause 2: Protestant ideas from Europe

Protestant ideas began in Europe, in the lands of the German princes. Criticisms of the Catholic Church spread slowly until 1517 when Martin Luther pinned ninety-five theses or arguments criticising the Catholic Church on the church door at Wittenberg. Luther's ideas spread rapidly and he became famous all over Europe as the leader of Protestantism. Most importantly, he won the support of many German princes, perhaps because he argued that the Church's wealth ought to be taken over by kings and princes. One king who did not agree with Luther was Henry VIII. Henry, who was not fond of writing, took the trouble to write a book defending the Catholic Church against Luther's criticisms. In the early 1520s Henry had no intention of leaving the Catholic Church.

Cause 3: Printing and the spread of ideas

By the 1530s printing had developed a long way since the days of William Caxton. There were many more printing presses but they were controlled by the Government. In England in the 1520s pamphlets were printed to attack the new Protestant ideas.

Then, in the 1530s, Thomas Cromwell, who organised the new Church of England, used printing to spread the new ideas. Printing allowed the new Bibles, written in English, to reach every church much quicker than if they had been written by hand.

Cause 4: Religion in England before 1530

Was it easier for Henry to change the country's religion because the people of England were unhappy about the Catholic Church?

In the 1520s they were still spending plenty of money on churches. Windows were reglazed, statues of saints were repainted or new ones were made, churches were enlarged and reroofed. In Bristol two churches were rivals, competing to see which one could build the larger and more decorated reredos – the screen behind the altar. Each instructed its builders to outbuild the other!

People were also still going on pilgrimages to Canterbury and Walsingham in Norfolk in large numbers. They were also giving money and land to the monasteries. In 1536 even Henry VIII founded a new monastery. Later that year Henry and Cromwell began to close the monasteries. This led to the Pilgrimage of Grace, a major rebellion in the North against Henry's changes.

Thomas Cranmer
Archbishop of Canterbury (from 1533 until his execution in Mary's reign in 1555).
Cranmer was a moderate man who did not want to punish people because they disagreed about the details of religion. He wrote the Prayer Book that has been used ever since.

Thomas Cromwell
Henry's brilliant chief adviser in the 1530s.
Cromwell worked very hard to make the country's government more efficient, as well as organizing the new Church of England. One of his greatest achievements was to order that Bibles in English instead of Latin should be in every parish church. He spent his own money having the Bible translated into English

CAUSES AND CONSEQUENCES: THE BEGINNING OF THE CHURCH OF ENGLAND

1   Which of the four causes were short-term causes and which were long-term causes of change?
2   How else could you divide the four causes into groups?
3   Was Cause 1 more or less important than Cause 2 in starting the Church of England? Explain your answer.
4   Was Cause 3 more or less important than Cause 4 in starting the Church of England? Explain your answer.
5   How did Causes 2 and 3 work together to produce religious change?
6   Which was the most important cause of religious change in England?
7   Was it inevitable that a Protestant Church would be started in England? Explain your answer.

An artist's version of the badge of the rebels who took part in the Pilgrimage of Grace. It shows the 5 wounds received by Christ on the cross.

Thomas More (on the right) was Henry's Chancellor but refused to agree to Henry's religious changes. However, most Tudor people thought that it was their duty to obey the king, even if they secretly disagreed with him. Many bishops wanted to stay Catholic but changed their religion because they obeyed the king, not their own conscience.

Edward VI and the Church of England (1547–1553).
Edward was only 9 when he followed his father, Henry VIII, as king. Edward had stronger Protestant beliefs. New laws made the church more Protestant and less moderate but this caused rebellions in 1549.

▓ The effects of religious change

Henry VIII: 1509–1547

For almost a thousand years England had been part of the Roman Catholic Church. Suddenly in 1534 it had its own Church and Henry replaced the Pope as its head. Everyone had to belong to the new Church of England.

Some people wanted to stay Catholics. The most famous objectors were Thomas More, who had been Henry's Chancellor, and John Fisher, Bishop of Rochester. Both men were executed in 1535 because they refused to accept Henry as the Head of the Church.

At first most people were not alarmed because church services did not change and churches looked as colourful as ever. The change seemed to be just a theory or idea. It did not affect people's lives in a practical way. Then, in 1536, Thomas Cromwell began to close monasteries all over England. This Dissolution of the Monasteries helped to cause a great rebellion, the Pilgrimage of Grace.

The pilgrims were northerners, rich and poor, men and women. Many had lost jobs in monasteries or on monastery farms. The poorest had depended on the monks for food and money. Now they wondered how they would survive. Others joined the rebellion because they did not want to leave the Roman Catholic Church. They hoped that the rebellion would change the king's mind or even replace Henry with his Catholic daughter, Mary, and return England to the Pope.

However, the rebellion failed. Henry promised to consider the rebels' demands so they went back to their homes. Then he rounded up the leaders and many were executed. No one dared to try again, even when it seemed that Catholic countries, France, Spain and Scotland, would invade England in 1539. Henry was so afraid that he had forts built all along the south coast. The attack never came.

PEOPLE IN THE PAST: CHOOSING KING OR CHURCH

1 How did people react to the changes in the 1530s?
2 Why did some English people rebel against Henry VIII in 1536?
3 Do you think it was easy for people to choose between their monarch and their religion?
4 Most people accepted the changes. Why did people like More and Fisher not accept them?

Mary Tudor: 1553–1558

Mary had stayed Catholic even though her father, Henry VIII, had changed the country's religion. When she became queen she changed the laws about religion. Suddenly England was a Catholic country again. Some Protestants refused to change their religion. Eight hundred escaped abroad. Others were executed by burning. Does this show that the people thought that their religion was important?

Source A

Some of the onlookers wept, others prayed to God to give Rogers strength to bear the pain. Others gathered the ashes and bones and wrapped them in paper to preserve them. These burnings may well cause a revolt.

(A letter by the Spanish ambassador, describing the first burning of a Protestant, John Rogers, in 1555)

Source B

On 4 February Rogers was carried between 10 and 11 o'clock into Smithfield and burned for his wrong opinions.

(Diary of Henry Machin, a Londoner who was a Catholic)

Source C

Capital punishment was common at the time. After the northern rebellion in 1569, 700 people were sentenced to hanging. Between 17 and 54 people were hanged every year in Essex, generally for small-scale theft. The risk of being executed in Tudor Nottinghamshire was roughly the same as being killed in a road accident today.

(Adapted from C. S. L. Davies, *Peace, Print and Protestantism: 1450–1558*, 1976)

Source D

About 280 people were burned during Mary's reign. About 230 were men and 51 women. This is a list of some of their jobs:

Men	Women
21 churchmen	32 work unknown
13 weavers	1 gentlewoman
9 gentlemen	2 servants
7 farmers	5 farmers' wives
6 labourers	2 millers' and
4 clothworkers	weavers' wives
3 brewers, tanners, sawyers	Also wives of brewers and shoemakers and the blind daughter of a ropemaker.
2 tailors, bricklayers, carpenters	

Others included shoemakers, painters, barbers, cooks and servants.

Source E

Women at their marketing, men at their daily trade, the cobbler at his bench, the ploughman trudging his farrow – all learnt to know the awful smell of burning human flesh, the flesh of a neighbour, of a man or woman as familiar as the village pump. That stench of human burning became an everyday experience.

(Adapted from H. F. M. Prescott, *Mary Tudor*, 1952)

The number of people burnt in each area

Source F

This map shows where people were executed in Mary's reign because they refused to accept the Catholic religion

Mary Tudor
Daughter of Henry VIII and Catherine of Aragon.
She kept to her mother's Catholic religion all her life.

DIFFERENT VIEWS: DEATH BY BURNING

1 Look at Sources A–F. Which sources would you use to support each of these statements?
   a People hated the burnings.
   b People did not hate the burnings.
2 Why might historians disagree about reactions to the burnings?
3 Do you think Source E is an accurate account of what it was like to live during Mary's reign?
4 Which of these statements do you agree with? Explain your choice.
   a Religion was very important to people.
   b Religion was very important to some people but not to most people

Elizabeth I: 1558–1603

These two pages tell you more about the ways religion affected people's lives. Does the evidence change your answer to question 4 on page 15?

Elizabeth was a Protestant. After she became queen everyone again became members of the Protestant Church of England. This made enemies of the Pope and Catholic countries like Spain. In 1570 the Pope excommunicated Elizabeth. This meant she was condemned to the tortures of hell after she died and that Catholics should not accept her as queen. Any Catholic who killed her was doing God's work. Some English people did plot against Elizabeth. They intended to make her Catholic cousin, Mary Queen of Scots, queen of both countries.

In 1587 the danger was so great that Elizabeth finally agreed to Mary's execution. The next year she faced the Spanish Armada. King Philip of Spain expected that many English people would fight against Elizabeth, especially in the North, where Catholicism was still strong. However, the Spanish navy was defeated, so English Catholics did not have to choose between their religion and their queen. Perhaps there was no need to worry. A preacher in Kent said that only one in ten people understood the basic ideas of Christianity. Most people went to church because they always had done.

Ireland was another danger. The Irish were still Catholic and Spain might use Ireland as a base for an invasion. How could England be safe from invasion from Ireland? It was impossible to change the religious ideas of the people – so the answer was to change the people! Many English and Scottish Protestants were given lands in Ulster, the north-east of Ireland. The English government hoped that these Protestants would stop Spain using Ireland as a base. However, this only created more enemies in Ireland because the Protestants were given lands belonging to Catholics.

Plots against Elizabeth

1569 Rebellion of the Northern Earls, a rebellion led by Catholics but caused by a mixture of reasons.

1570 The Pope excommunicated Elizabeth.

1571 The Ridolfi plot. Supported by Spain, it aimed to make Mary Queen of Scots queen of England.

1583 The Throckmorton Plot. Supported by Spain, it also aimed to make Mary queen of England.

1586 The Babington Plot. A group of Catholics led by Anthony Babington planned to rescue Mary from prison, kill Elizabeth and make Mary queen.

1587 Mary Queen of Scots was executed.

1588 The Spanish Armada (later Armadas in 1596, 1597 and 1599)

The inside of a parish church before the Reformation. Compare this with the picture opposite. What changes did people see in their churches? Why did people think these changes were important?

Civil wars

Differences in religion caused more changes in the seventeenth century. Many people, both Puritans (extreme Protestants) and Catholics, could not worship God in the way they wanted. Some of them were so desperate that they decided to emigrate to America, a land Europeans still knew very little about. The Pilgrim Fathers were Puritans who emigrated in the *Mayflower* in 1620. They wanted to start again, with their own religion and religious rules, free from interference by the king.

Other people were not so worried about religion. In the 1640s people in the Lake District were described as 'ignorant and blind as to religion'. One old man talked of seeing a play where 'there was a man on a tree and blood ran down'. That was all he knew about Jesus Christ.

When the Civil War began in England in 1642 religion was one of the causes. Many Protestants, especially the Puritans, believed that Charles I and the Archbishop of Canterbury, William Laud, were moving the Church of England back towards Catholicism. So, when the Civil War began, Puritans were on the side of Parliament, fighting against the king. People who liked Catholic ideas were more likely to fight for the king.

James II lost his throne in 1688 partly because of his religion. He was a Catholic but most of the important people in the country were Protestants. When James became king he began to give important jobs to other Catholics. Protestants feared these changes. They were worried they might also lose their lands to Catholics, and that James would force everyone to change their religion. They threatened to rebel and then invited a Protestant, William of Orange, to be king (as William III). In 1688 James fled, but was able to win support among Catholics in Ireland until his army was beaten by William III at the Battle of the Boyne in 1690.

Puritans were extreme Protestants who wanted to make their religion as simple or 'pure' as possible. They wore plain, dark clothing and disliked entertainments such as dancing and theatres. In Elizabeth's reign Puritans wanted all the theatres closed down. They thought people should be reading the Bible instead.

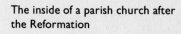

The inside of a parish church after the Reformation

John Wesley (1703–1791)
He spent his life travelling to tell people the story of God and Christ. His 'method' was to use ordinary people as preachers at services and he said that people should pray and read the Bible together regularly. He wanted to stay part of the Church of England but eventually his followers began their own church – the Methodists. His brother, Charles, wrote many famous hymns.

The importance of religion

Religion was an important part of life in Britain between 1500 and 1750. For most of this time, the Government said that everybody had to go to church and told them exactly what services to use. Therefore, everybody saw some of the effects of the religious changes because the churches looked very different after the Reformation. They were much less colourful and the services were different. Rebels in Devon and Cornwall in 1549 did not like the new Protestant service because people joined in with the priest and it was in English instead of Latin. They said it was like 'a Christmas game'.

Many people died because they disagreed with the king or queen about religion. Others thought it was more important to obey the monarch than follow their own beliefs. Many lords and officials who had worked for Henry VIII,

continued to work for Mary and then Elizabeth, saying it was their duty to change religion if the king or queen changed. Many ordinary people did not rebel because they did not understand the details of the religious changes. Earning a living was more important.

In 1500 there had been only one Christian religion in Britain – Roman Catholicism. Then the Church of England began, but different Protestant groups disagreed with each other. Puritans and other dissenters criticised the Church of England almost as much as they criticised the Pope and Catholics. The growth of Methodism in the eighteenth century showed that many people were still dissatisfied with their Church. There were still complaints about the riches of the bishops and laziness of the priests, just as there always had been.

Churches looked very different and the monasteries were closed.

Religion caused civil wars and the deposition of kings.

Religious differences helped to cause wars with other countries.

The effects of religious changes

England, Scotland and Ireland had different religions.

Many people were executed or imprisoned because of their beliefs.

People emigrated so they could worship in freedom.

SUMMARY: RELIGION 1500–1750

1   This chapter began with the story of Margaret Clitherow. Why did some people die for their religion when most others accepted the changes?

2   Were the changes in religion important to the people of Britain? Give reasons for your answer.

3   Look at your version of the chart on page 8. Amend or add to the answers you put into the chart at the beginning of this investigation. Do you want to

alter your answer about the importance of the changes in religion?

4   Look back to the list of causes of change on page 8. Which of the causes were the most important in changing religion?

5   Do you think religion had helped to unite the people of Britain by 1750?

6   Do you think that the religious changes of 1500–1750 still affect us today?

THE POWER OF MONARCH AND PARLIAMENT

In the summer of 1642 people were expecting a war to start. It was not a war abroad, against another country, it was a war in England between Englishmen. For two years the king, Charles I, and Parliament had been quarrelling about taxes, religion and whether the king could rule without calling Parliament at all. Neither side would give in. Civil War began.

The Verney family was a well-off gentry family from Buckinghamshire. Sir Edmund Verney and three of his sons supported the King. Sir Edmund had been one of Charles I's officials for many years. Even so, Sir Edmund had thought hard about what to do. He wrote to a friend:

'I do not like the quarrel, and do heartily wish that the king would yield and consent to what they desire. I have eaten his bread and served him near thirty years, and will not do so base a thing as to forsake him; and choose rather to lose my life (which I am sure that I shall do).'

But there was worse to come for the Verney family. Sir Edmund's eldest son, Ralph, chose to fight on the other side, for Parliament, even though this meant fighting against his own family. 'Mun' Verney wrote to his brother, Ralph:

'It grieves my heart that my father and I should be your enemy. I am so much troubled to think of your being on the side that you are that I can write no more, only I shall pray for peace.'

Mun's prayers did not work. His father, Sir Edmund, was killed at the Battle of Edgehill in 1642. The

Verneys were only one of thousands of families who were torn apart by the Civil War.

The Civil War was the most obvious conflict between the monarch and Parliament, but arguments about their power carried on throughout the years 1500 to 1750. In this chapter you will be answering this question:

● ***How and why did the power of the monarch and Parliament change?***

Sir Edmund Verney

Think about the Verneys. What does their story tell us about the importance of the quarrel between king and Parliament? Why do you think the king and Parliament quarrelled?

King Charles I opened the Civil War by raising his standard at Nottingham on 22 August 1642

Kings and queens of England: 1485–1760

Before we start to find out how the power of the monarch changed you should answer the questions below. They will help you to find out about some of the people who helped to bring about these changes and to work out some of the important things which happened.

KINGS AND QUEENS

1 Draw a timeline showing all the monarchs from the family tree below and when they reigned.
2 There was a period when there was no monarch. When was this? Why did it happen?
3 a Which of the monarchs on pages 20–21 do you think were successful?
  b Which were unsuccessful?
  c Why do you think some monarchs were more successful than others?
4 In 1760 George II died and his grandson became King George III. What advice would you have given him on how he should be a good king?

The kings and queens of England 1485–1760

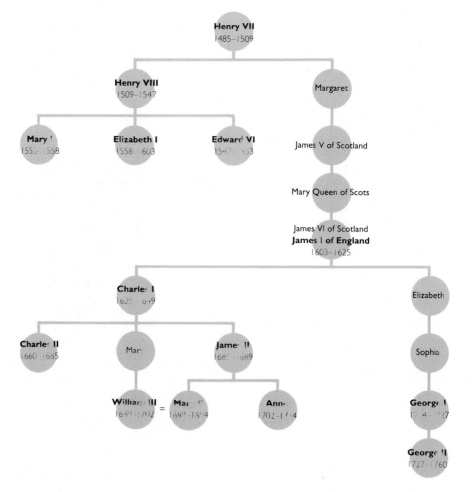

Henry VII
1485–1509

Henry VIII
1509–1547

Margaret

Mary
1553–1558

Elizabeth I
1558–1603

Edward VI
1547–1553

James V of Scotland

Mary Queen of Scots

James VI of Scotland
James I of England
1603–1625

Charles I
1625–1649

Elizabeth

Charles II
1660–1685

Mary

James II
1685–1689

Sophia

William III
1689–1702 = Mary II
1689–1694

Anne
1702–1714

George I
1714–1727

George II
1727–1760

Henry VII (1485–1509)

Henry VII (1485–1509)

Henry VII became king after he defeated Richard III at the Battle of Bosworth. He stopped the quarrels between the nobles and made England much more peaceful. Some people thought that he was mean but he was the only monarch in this period not to die in debt. This was because he avoided war.

Henry VIII (1509–1547)

Henry VIII was only seventeen when he became king. He was very clever and a good sportsman. After Henry began the Church of England he closed all the monasteries and confiscated their lands. This should have made him very rich but he spent the money on war with France. Henry could be very harsh. He executed anyone who opposed him, including two of his wives whom he suspected of being unfaithful.

Elizabeth I (1558–1603)

At the start of her reign England was poor and weak but by 1603 English ships had defeated the Spanish Armada and English merchants traded all over the world. She chose a moderate form of Protestant religion which was accepted by most people. She selected her advisers wisely and never married because her husband would have taken over as king. English people did not want her to marry a foreigner, but if she chose an Englishman this would have caused jealousy among many lords.

Charles I (1625–1649)

Charles I was a quiet, shy man. He trusted his friends completely but upset many of the important people. They felt he would not take advice from them, only from his favourites. Many people also distrusted him because they thought he was trying to bring back the Catholic religion. Charles also quarrelled with his Parliaments and in 1642 this quarrel turned into civil war. Although Charles lost the Civil War he would not agree to the terms made by Parliament. He tried to get his enemies to fight among themselves so he could get his power back. In 1649 Parliament put him on trial and had him executed.

Oliver Cromwell

Oliver Cromwell was one of the strongest critics of King Charles I. When the Civil War broke out he formed his own regiment, the Ironsides, to fight for Parliament. He became one of the leading generals and agreed to the execution of Charles I. In 1653 the army took control of the country and Cromwell was made Lord Protector. His army and navy made England powerful again but he had to raise high taxes to pay for this. In 1657, Parliament tried to make Cromwell king but he refused. He died in 1658. A year later the English decided to bring back Charles I's son as king.

Charles II (1660–1685)

After his father's execution Charles went to Scotland, where he was proclaimed king. He tried to retake England but was defeated by Cromwell at the Battle of Worcester in 1651. He spent the next six weeks hiding, on one occasion in an oak tree while the soldiers searched for him underneath. In 1660 he was invited to return as king. He had to be careful how he ruled if he wanted to stay king. He seemed to be easy-going but he could be cruel to those who opposed him. Although he was in favour of the Catholic Church, he kept his beliefs secret until he was dying.

James II (1685–1689)

Unlike his brother, James II was openly a Catholic. This upset many people who were afraid he would try to make England into a Catholic country and rule without Parliament. Like his father, he was determined to have his own way. Some important politicians decided to invite James's son-in-law, William of Orange, to be king. When William invaded, James had very few supporters, even among English Catholics, and he fled to France rather than risk execution.

William and Mary (1689–1702)

William III was Dutch. He only agreed to become king of England because he wanted England to fight in his war against the French. He was accepted by the English because he was a Protestant and because he was married to James II's Protestant daughter, Mary (who died in 1694). Although William wanted to be a powerful king, he was often away from England, looking after his Dutch subjects or fighting against the French. While he was king, Parliament gained much more power.

George II (1727–1760)

For the first ten years of George II's reign his decisions were influenced by his clever wife Queen Caroline. She persuaded him to keep Robert Walpole as Prime Minister and Walpole gave England many years of peace and prosperity. Towards the end of his reign, England was involved in wars and George II was helped by another able Prime Minister, William Pitt the elder. George II was a conscientious king, reading and signing personally all the important paperwork. He was also the last king of England to lead his army into battle, at Dettingen in 1743.

Charles II (1660–1685)

James II (1685–1688)

Kings, queens and Parliament

1215 – Magna Carta: When the barons rebelled against King John they forced him to agree to a set of rules about how he would govern the country. John very quickly ended the agreement.

1280s – Edward I often needed money for wars in Wales and Scotland and against France. He started to call Parliaments regularly to get agreement for his taxes.

1327 – Edward II was the first king since 1066 to be deposed – forced to give up his crown. He had tried to rule without taking advice from the most important nobles.

1450s – Henry VI was a disaster as king. Even so, people did not want to depose him because they still believed kings were chosen by God. He was only deposed after twenty-four years of being a poor king.

These pages give you an overview of the power of the monarch – the king or queen – and Parliament between 1066 and 1750. In 1066 William the Conqueror was all-powerful and there was no such thing as Parliament.

The king made all the decisions even though he asked others for advice. However, he did not *have* to consult anyone.

The king was more powerful because he controlled England and part of France.

The king was God's representative. This was shown by God giving William his first victory at Hastings.

William owned all the land. Everyone, even barons, depended upon him for their land.

The king needed the support of his barons to control the country, especially in the north and south-west.

The king had the power of life and death over everyone. He could decide any law case and punishment.

Everyone was expected to fight for the king.

Barons

King

The balance of power: William the Conqueror and the barons in 1066

The power of the king in 1500

In 1500 England was ruled by King Henry VII. He made all the major decisions with the help of advisers he chose himself. He only needed Parliament when he wanted taxes or when he wanted to get the backing of the country for new laws. Henry was king for twenty-four years. During that time there were only seven Parliaments, which met for a total of fifty-nine weeks.

People still wanted a strong king to defend them from foreign attackers and to keep law and order. However, King Henry had to be careful. In the previous hundred years three English kings had been killed and replaced after rebellions by the nobles. The most powerful people in the country expected the king to listen to them and to follow policies they agreed with.

WHO GOVERNED THE COUNTRY?

1 What were the main changes in the king's power between 1066 and 1500?
2 What were the main changes in the king's power between 1500 and 1750?
3 Draw a set of scales showing the power of the monarch and Parliament for:
   a 1500 b today

The king could not rule without Parliament. He had to call Parliament because:

- Parliament renewed his income each year
- there had to be a general election at least every seven years – this meant that he could not run the country without a Parliament
- the king had to choose ministers who could work with Parliament – this meant that Parliament could force the king to dismiss a minister

The king chose his own ministers. He could give titles and good jobs to those who supported him. This way he could get many members of Parliament on his side.

King

Parliament

The balance of power:
George II and Parliament
in 1750

What was Parliament?

From the time of William the Conqueror the king summoned the most powerful men in the country, the lords and the bishops, to give them his instructions and to ask for their advice. In the thirteenth century he also began to invite representatives of the main towns and of the smaller landowners. These meetings were called Parliaments. By 1500 the form of Parliament had become fixed. The House of Lords was made up of the lords – the biggest landowners – and the bishops. The representatives of the main towns and the smaller landowners made up the House of Commons.

Each county elected two MPs. Only men who owned land could vote or become MPs. Each town could decide for itself how it chose its two MPs. In the early seventeenth century about a quarter of adult men could vote.

 ## When were the turning-points?

Sometimes changes take place gradually over a long period of time. At other times they take place quite quickly. When there is an important change over a short period of time we call that moment of change a turning-point. In the next four pages you can investigate some possible turning-points in the relationship between monarch and Parliament.

Copy the grid below into your book then fill it in as you work through the next four pages. In the top row put an arrow pointing upwards if you think the monarch gained more power. Put an arrow downwards if you think the monarch lost power to Parliament. In the bottom row enter a number to show how important you think that change was: 0 = not important, 1 = important, 2 = very important. When you have completed the grid answer these questions:

- Which was the most important turning-point?
- What evidence would you use to support your answer?

	1 1530s	2 Elizabeth	3 Charles I	4 1660	5 1688–9	6 William III	7 After 1714
King's power							
Importance of turning point							

Turning-point 1: the 1530s

King Henry VIII was a very powerful king. Was he more powerful than his predecessors?

Henry VIII was Head of the Church. He could decide what his subjects should believe. No medieval king could do this.

Henry could only govern England with the help of nobles and other landowners. The best way of getting their support for his plans was through Parliament.

Henry VIII

Henry had the power to make war against foreign countries but he could only pay for wars with taxes. He could only get these taxes from Parliament.

Henry made himself Head of the Church but he used Parliament to make this legal. Parliament passed the laws which gave Henry control of the Church.

Turning-point 2: Elizabeth I

Elizabeth I was queen at a time when the job of ruling was traditionally done by men. How successful was she? Did the crown gain power or lose it during her reign? Look at the details on the left.

Elizabeth's power

● Elizabeth made all the decisions about governing England. She listened to advisers but did not have to agree with them.

● Elizabeth could call and dismiss Parliament whenever she wished, but she needed Parliaments to agree to taxes.

● Parliament criticized Elizabeth about religion and because she did not marry. Sometimes Elizabeth ended parliaments because of these criticisms before they gave her taxes.

● Elizabeth did not marry. The people did not want her to marry a foreigner who might change English policies. If she married an English nobleman it would cause jealousy amongst the rest.

CHANGES: HENRY VIII AND ELIZABETH

1 What were the changes in the monarch's power in the 1500s?
2 What were the changes in Parliament's power in the 1500s?
3 Was Henry VIII more or less powerful than medieval kings?
4 Was Elizabeth more or less powerful than Henry VIII?
5 Now fill in your copy of the chart on page 23.

Turning-point 3: Charles I

In 1640 Charles I was forced to call a Parliament. He was at war with Scotland and he had run out of money. The only way he could get more money was to ask Parliament for taxes. Members of Parliament who did not like the way the king was running the country tried to force him to change his policies. Two important laws were passed:

● The Triennial Act, 1641. The king had to call a new Parliament within three years of the end of the previous one. He could not go for long periods without holding a Parliament.

● Act against dissolving the present Parliament without its consent, 1641.

Charles I could not end this Parliament unless it agreed.

Until this time the monarch had the right to call and dismiss Parliament whenever he or she wished. In 1641, Parliament forced Charles I to agree to these changes because he was short of money and could only get it from Parliament.

In the end, Charles felt that he could not surrender any more of his powers. He chose to go to war against those who were trying to control him but he lost the war and he was executed. The monarchy was abolished and Parliament governed the country for eleven years.

King Charles I walking to his place of execution

Turning-point 4: Charles II, 1660

The monarchy was restored in 1660 because people wanted a king as well as a parliament.

When Charles II became king no conditions or rules were laid down. In one way Charles was king on the same terms as his father had been before the Parliament of 1640. However, he knew that he had to be careful if he wanted to keep his throne. Charles had to agree to many laws which he personally did not like.

On the other hand, no one wanted another civil war. Charles II's mistakes were blamed on his ministers and he took full advantage of this. When someone said of him that 'he never said a foolish thing and never did a wise one', he replied, 'My words are my own but my actions are those of my ministers.'

In the last four years of his reign he was able to manage without parliaments altogether, with the help of money given to him by King Louis XIV of France.

CHANGES: CHARLES I AND CHARLES II

1   How did the Acts of 1641 change the power of the monarch?
2   Why did Charles I agree to those changes?
3   Charles II was restored without any rules about governing. Does this mean that there had been no change in the monarch's power?
4   Now fill in your chart.

Turning-point 5: 1688–9

1685 James, a Catholic, became king. Protestants accepted him as king because they thought he would be succeeded by one of his Protestant daughters, Mary or Anne. His first Parliament gave him an income for life. He used this to build up a permanent army in England.

1687 James wanted Catholics to have important jobs in the Government and the army. There were laws against this and Parliament would not change them. James issued a Declaration of Indulgence to free Catholics from these laws.

1688 James and his Catholic wife had a son. Many people feared that James would use the army to do away with Parliament and try to 'make England a Catholic country.

1688 A group of English lords invited James's son-in-law, William of Orange, to take control of the country. James escaped to France.

1689 Parliament declared William and his wife Mary joint sovereigns.

William of Orange (William III)

James II hears of William III's landing

Turning-point 6: William III

The reign of William III saw important changes in the relationship between monarch and Parliament. Look at the following points:

William was elected king by Parliament. In 1701 Parliament passed the Act of Settlement which excluded James II's son and all Catholics from the throne of England. Parliament was able to decide who should be monarch.

Parliament only met for a few weeks each year. The monarch was still expected to make the important decisions and run the country.

William of Orange

England was at war during most of William's reign. To pay for this he needed taxes but Parliament would only give him taxes for one year. He had to go to Parliament at least once a year.

William could still refuse to pass laws which had been agreed by both Houses of Parliament.

William sometimes had to choose ministers he did not like because they could get Parliament to grant taxes.

JAMES II AND WILLIAM OF ORANGE

1 Was James II a powerful king? Think about the following points when answering this question:
   - Parliament gave him an income for life.
   - He had a permanent army in peace time.
   - He could excuse groups of people from obeying the law.
   - There was a successful rebellion against him.
2 How did William's wars affect his power as king?
3 William III thought that he was as powerful as his predecessors. Do you think he was right?
4 Now fill in your chart.

Turning-point 7: After 1714

In 1714 Queen Anne died. Her successor, George I, was already the ruler of a German state called Hanover, where he did not have to consult a Parliament. Both George I (1714–27) and his son George II (1727–60) expected to make all the important decisions and to appoint and dismiss their ministers as they pleased. However, they ruled England differently from their predecessors for a number of reasons:

Robert Walpole

For twenty years (1722–42) Robert Walpole was chief or Prime Minister to George I and George II. Walpole was a very clever man and the kings relied on his advice. He was very good at getting support for government policy in Parliament.

From George I onwards monarchs no longer refused to agree to new laws passed by Parliament.

The king and his ministers gave jobs to MPs who supported them. This made it possible to get Parliaments which supported the king's policies.

Walpole was in charge of the treasury which had a lot of jobs that could be given to people in exchange for their support. The kings insisted on making these appointments but relied on Walpole's knowledge to give them to the right people.

In 1742 Walpole lost his majority in Parliament. King George II was forced to accept his resignation. In 1757 George II was forced to appoint William Pitt as Prime Minister because of pressure from Parliament.

George II

George I and George II preferred to spend their time in Hanover. They did not attend many meetings of their ministers (cabinet). They still made decisions but could not influence the discussions of their ministers.

CHANGES AFTER 1714

1 Why were the king's ministers more important after 1714 than they had been before?
2 Did Parliament gain any power during the reigns of the first two Georges?
3 Which of the following statements do you think describes the situation at the end of George II's reign?

a The monarch was more powerful than Parliament.
b Parliament was more powerful than the monarch.
c Monarch and Parliament were equally powerful.
4 Now fill in your chart.

Why did the power of the monarch change: 1500–1750?

Historians do not simply describe what happened in the past. They also try to explain why those things happened. One reason alone is not enough to explain why a particular change took place; the historian has to look at several causes. Below you can see three possible reasons why the power of the monarch changed.

Personality

The actions, personality and talents of individual kings and queens could affect the relationship between the monarch and Parliament. For instance, Henry VIII wanted to divorce Catherine of Aragon and make himself Head of the Church. This made him much more powerful but, because he used Parliament to pass the laws, this also increased Parliament's power and created problems for his successors.

Religion

The changes in religion helped to change the power of the monarch. If the monarch made religious changes which were popular, this increased their power. If the monarch tried to make unpopular religious changes, people might turn against them. James II was a Catholic at a time when the English people did not want a Catholic king. His attempts to give important jobs to Catholics led to him losing his throne.

Wars

The need of the monarch to fight wars affected her/his relationship with Parliament. A popular war might rally support behind the monarch. However, wars cost a lot of money. A monarch might have to agree to Parliament's wishes in exchange for taxes. Charles I's war with Scotland forced him to call the Long Parliament in 1640. He then had to agree to many things which he did not like.

The Gunpowder Plot
This group of men plotted to blow up the king and Parliament in 1605 to free Catholics from the laws made against their religion.

Bates
Robert Winter
Christopher Wright
Iohn Wright
Thomas Percy
Guido Fawkes
Robert Catesby
Th. W.

Other reasons

The three reasons on page 28 were not the only ones that were important. Other events and changes in the period 1500 to 1750 may have affected the relationship between monarch and Parliament.

Printing and newspapers

The invention of the printing press in the middle of the fifteenth century meant that new ideas and criticisms of the Government spread to many people. Governments soon realised this and tried to control the books which were printed and imposed severe penalties on those who printed books and pamphlets illegally. However, printing presses were small and easy to hide and to move around. This made it difficult to stop the spread of new ideas. In 1500 there were probably twenty million printed books in the world. By 1600 this figure had probably risen to two hundred million.

During the Civil War thousands of pamphlets and hundreds of newspapers were published putting forward all sorts of ideas. During the eighteenth century, politicians made use of the newspapers to criticise each other.

Education

In the Middle Ages very few people went to school. This changed rapidly after 1400. The invention of printing and the translation of the Bible into English meant that many more people wanted to be able to read. Schools were set up in most towns throughout the country. By the beginning of the seventeenth century most landowners sent their sons to the local grammar school and then to university. Many studied law although they did not all become lawyers. Most of the Members of Parliament who challenged Charles I had been to university and had been trained in the law. They wanted a bigger say in the government of the country.

New ideas

The growth of education and the spread of books encouraged new ideas about how countries should be governed. Some people said that more people should be given a say in how they were governed. Others argued that there was no need for a monarch. These new ideas were very common in England during the period 1649–60. They did not always lead to a reduction in the power of the crown. Many of the gentry thought that these ideas were very dangerous. They wanted to strengthen the monarch's power to stop such ideas spreading. This helped to strengthen the power of Charles II after the Restoration.

An engraving of an early printing press

CAUSES: WHY DID THE MONARCH'S POWER CHANGE?

1 Look back through this chapter. Find 3 examples of individuals who increased or decreased the power of the Crown.
2 Find 3 examples of religious matters affecting the power of the Crown.
3 Find 3 examples of wars affecting the power of the Crown.
4 **a** Which cause do you think was the most important in reducing the power of the monarch?
   b Which cause do you think was the least important in reducing the power of the monarch?
   c What evidence can you find to support your answers?
5 Use one or more of the six factors on these pages to explain why Parliament became more powerful between 1500 and 1750.
6 Look back to your answers to the questions on page 8. Do you need to change or amend those answers now?

Monarch, Parliament and people

Between 1500 and 1750 there was a great change in the government of the country. Parliament became far more important. By 1750 it shared the government with the monarch instead of only meeting when the monarch wanted it. This was a very important stage in the history of Parliament and it is very important for us because nowadays Parliament decides our laws and the monarch has very little power at all. But did this change matter to the people who lived at the time?

Elections

For most of this period of history the monarch decided when they wanted to consult Parliament and ordered an election. After 1694 elections had to be held at least every three years. In 1716 this was extended to seven years to allow governments more time to work.

A polling station in the 1700s. How is this different to a polling station today?

Each county, except Yorkshire, sent two members to Parliament. Yorkshire sent six because it was so big. Many towns also sent members to Parliament. Most of these were in the south of England because these had been the most important towns when Parliament started in the thirteenth century.

The Government and the great landowners were often able to arrange who the candidates were.

They made sure the candidates were government supporters. They also arranged that, if two MPs were needed, there were only two candidates. This meant that in many places there was no election and people did not have a chance to vote.

Voting was done in public. The voter went up on to a platform, called out his own name and then called out the names of his chosen candidates. Voters could easily be bribed or intimidated because everyone knew how they had voted.

Who voted?

Nowadays every man and woman over the age of eighteen can vote. Between 1500 and 1750 it was very different:

- Only men could vote.
- In the counties a man had to own land worth at least forty shillings a year to be able to vote. This excluded those who only rented land, even if they were quite well off.
- The towns decided for themselves how they would elect their Members of Parliament. There was a great variety of systems. In some towns almost all the men had the right to vote. In others the vote could be restricted to the owners of certain plots of land. If one person owned all these plots he could choose the Members of Parliament by himself.

Historians think that about one quarter of the men had the right to vote. These were generally the richest people. Even then not all of them were given the chance to vote because, as you have read above, there were often not enough candidates to have an election.

Did it matter?

Most people in England in the period 1500–1750 worked on the land. They were mostly concerned with the immediate needs of daily life, such as whether they had enough food or could afford to buy another cow. Most were too poor to pay much tax and the Government did little to help them. There was no social security, no state education, no National Health Service. For most of them it did not matter whether the monarch or Parliament made the decisions. Some decisions, however, did matter to ordinary people.

● Everyone went to church and so the way in which services were conducted mattered to them, as can be seen from the rebellions against religious changes in 1536 and 1549.

● The closing of the monasteries took away a refuge for the poor and unemployed, forcing them on to the roads and into the towns. Eventually the Government was forced to pass laws to help these people. The ruling class felt that large numbers of unemployed people wandering around the country were a threat to law and order. Both Crown and Parliament worked together to try to deal with this problem.

● The Government needed more and more money. This meant that taxes were higher and were asked for more often.

● The Civil War affected people throughout the country. Many joined, or were forced to join, the armies. As the armies moved around the country they forced the people to provide them with food and lodging. The people of towns taken after a siege were often treated very harshly.

It was believed that the monarch's touch could cure the disease of Scrofula, known as 'the King's Evil'. English monarchs regularly held sessions when victims of the disease were brought to be touched. This was last done in the reign of Queen Anne.

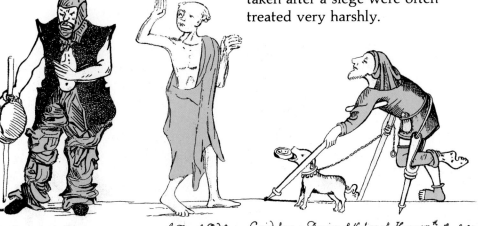

A Soap-eater, copied from a rare print of the time of Queen Elizabeth

A Tom of Bedlam copied from an old Drawing of the time of Edw: 6 in the possession of Fran: Douce Esq

Copied from a Drawing of the time of Henry VIII in the possession of Francis Douce, Esq.

Various types of beggar
These pictures were first drawn in the Tudor period. Wandering beggars were whipped, branded or hanged if they would not stay in their home villages or towns.

SUMMARY: PEOPLE IN THE PAST – MONARCH, PARLIAMENT AND PEOPLE

1　How were elections in the past different from elections today?

2　Did everyone have the same ideas about the changing power of the monarch and Parliament? Explain your answer. It may help to look back to the story of the Verneys on page 19.

3　Look back to your version of the chart on page 8.

　a　Amend or add to the answers you put into the chart at the beginning of this investigation.

　b　Do you want to alter your answer about the power of the monarch?

4　Do you think that the changes in the power of the monarch and Parliament had helped to unite Britain by 1750?

5　Do you think that the changes between 1500 and 1750 still affect us today?

CHOOSING SIDES: 1640–1660

Events 1625–42

1625 Charles I became king.
His first Parliament refuses to grant him the money he asks for.
Charles marries Henrietta Maria, a French princess and a Catholic.

1628 Parliament presents Charles with the Petition of Right, which criticises the way he is running the country.

1629 Charles dissolves Parliament. It does not meet again for eleven years.

1633 William Laud becomes Archbishop of Canterbury. He begins to make changes in religion which seem to be close to Catholicism.

1637 Charles tries to impose these religious changes on Scotland. This leads to war with Scotland.

1639 Charles makes the Earl of Strafford his chief minister.

1640 Charles is forced to call a Parliament to raise money for his war with Scotland.

1641 The Earl of Strafford is accused of treason by Parliament and executed.
Laws are passed limiting the king's powers.

1642 Civil War breaks out.

Chapter 3 investigated the way the power of the Crown and Parliament changed between 1500 and 1750. That overview did not give you the chance to investigate any of the events in detail. This chapter looks more closely at the Civil War. Think back to the arguments of the Verney family.

● *King or Parliament – which side would you have supported?*

◎ The king's view

Charles I believed that he had been appointed by God to be king and that this gave him special rights and duties. The name given to this view of kingship was the 'Divine Right of Kings'. This is how King Charles *might* have reflected on his reasons for going to war with Parliament the night before his execution:

'Being king is the greatest honour God could have given me. It is also a great responsibility because I have had to look after the people of England for God.

When I became king there were many problems but Parliament would not give me the money I needed to run the country. It was my job to decide about religion and foreign affairs but Parliament kept interfering. In 1628 they forced me to agree to the Petition of Right before they would give me any money.

I ruled for eleven years without a Parliament. Then I quarrelled with my Scottish subjects over religion and they invaded England. I was forced to call a Parliament. The MPs were angry that I had gone so long without a Parliament. They falsely accused my friend and chief adviser, the Earl of Strafford, of treason and executed him. Then they passed laws limiting my powers. I was becoming a puppet king; people still called me 'Your Majesty' but I had to take orders from Parliament.

I tried to deal with the traitors who persuaded the MPs to take away my rights and powers but they escaped. I had no choice but to appeal to the people of England to help me regain my proper rights and powers by making war on Parliament.'

◎ Parliament's view

Parliament's view of the conflict was rather different. The following extracts from contemporary documents will help you to understand the point of view of the king's critics.

Source A

To the King's Most Excellent Majesty,

It is declared by a law of King Edward the First that there should be no taxes without the agreement of Parliament. In the reign of King Edward the Third it was declared that no person should be forced to make any loans to the king against his will. By the good laws of this country your subjects have this freedom, that they should not be made to pay any tax or other charge not agreed to in Parliament.

Yet, recently, some people have been asked to lend money to your Majesty. When they have refused they have been ordered to appear before your Privy Council and some of them have been imprisoned against the laws of the country.

(The Petition of Right, 1628)

Source B

I shall explain to you the grievances which afflict the country under three headings. Firstly there is the attack on the liberties of Parliament, secondly there are the changes in religion and thirdly there are the attacks on our property.

Firstly, Parliament was dissolved before our complaints were heard; several gentlemen were imprisoned for speaking freely in Parliament.

Secondly, there have been changes in matters of religion ... the introduction of Popish ceremonies, of altars, bowing towards the east, pictures, crosses, cruxifixes and the like.

Thirdly, there is the attack on our property. The taking of taxes, without any grant or law.

(Speech by John Pym, 17 April 1640)

Source C

Whereas the House of Commons have impeached Thomas Earl of Strafford of high treason, for trying to introduce a tyrannical government against the law and advising His Majesty that he had an army in Ireland which he might use to bring this kingdom to order. Be it therefore enacted that he shall suffer such pains of death ...

(Act for the Attainder of the Earl of Strafford, 10 May 1641)

Source D

Parliament was forced to present the king with a petition on the state of the kingdom, in which they told him only as much of the truth as he could take, and complained only of his bad ministers; but this, instead of correcting him, made him more angry.

(Lucy Hutchinson, *Memoirs of the Life of Colonel John Hutchinson*)

Lucy Hutchinson
Wife of Colonel John Hutchinson. She wrote a biography of her husband to justify the part he played in the Civil War and the execution of Charles I.

John Pym (1583–1643) One of the leaders of the House of Commons who criticised Charles I.

CAUSES AND CONSEQUENCES: WHY THEY WENT TO WAR

1 Why did the king go to war?
2 Why did Parliament oppose the king?
3 Why do you think many people found it difficult to decide whom to support?
4 Who would you support? Explain your reasons fully.

The Civil War

After the Battle of Marston Moor some royalist prisoners were held in a local church. Their Parliamentarian guards passed the time by carving this picture of the king on the church door. It seems to show a snake wearing a crown. The carving, which is 82mm high, can still be seen on the church door.

1642

In the summer of 1642 both the king and Parliament began to organise their armies. Charles tried unsuccessfully to seize the port of Hull. On 22 August he raised his flag at Nottingham and called on the people for support. He began by moving towards the Welsh border where he had many supporters and he expected more men to join his army. Then he started to move back towards London which was controlled by Parliament. The first main battle was at Edgehill, north of Oxford. Prince Rupert, the king's nephew, chased the Parliamentarian cavalry off the battlefield but neither side gained any real advantage. The king continued towards London. Several miles west of the capital, at Turnham Green, he was met by the city's own armed force. Charles decided not to risk a battle and withdrew to Oxford for the winter.

1643

Charles had to capture London to win the war. In 1643 he tried to make a three-pronged attack on London from his bases in the north and west of England. His armies were not well-enough organised and the plan failed. Parliament was worried, however, and made an alliance with the Scots to obtain help against Charles in the north of England.

1644

In 1644 a joint Scottish and Parliamentarian army defeated Prince Rupert at Marston Moor near York. This was partly due to the better organisation of the Parliamentarian army and the generalship of one of their cavalry commanders, Oliver Cromwell. This defeat cut the king off from many of his supporters in the north of England. The king's forces were able, however, to hold off Parliamentarian attacks in the south and west of the country.

1645

Cromwell and some of his friends realised that they would only win the war if they had a better army. The New Model Army, which was created by Parliament, was a properly paid professional force. It was better disciplined and better trained than before. Charles was defeated by the New Model Army at Naseby in 1645.

1646

Although the war dragged on for another year, the King was running out of money and could not carry on much longer. In 1646 he decided to give up the fight. He slipped quietly out of Oxford and made his way north to Newark where he surrendered to the Scottish army.

1647—8

The Scots handed Charles over to Parliament. He managed to escape to the Isle of Wight, but was caught and kept a prisoner in Carisbrooke Castle. From there he plotted to get his enemies to fight against each other. The second Civil War lasted only a few months and Charles's friends were defeated again. It was enough, however, to persuade Cromwell and some other army officers that it was useless negotiating with the king. They forced Parliament to put him on trial.

England during the Civil War

NEWCASTLE ●

MARSTON MOOR ✕   YORK ●

●HULL

MANCHESTER ●

●CHESTER

●NEWARK

Royalist areas

BIRMINGHAM ●
NASEBY ✕

✕ Edgehill

Parliamentarian areas

●GLOUCESTER
●OXFORD

LONDON

ISLE OF WIGHT

THE CIVIL WAR

1 There were several events of the Civil War which might be regarded as turning-points in Charles's fortunes:
- his failure to seize Hull
- turning back at Turnham Green
- the Battle of Marston Moor
- the forming of the New Model Army

2 Which of these do you think was the key point at which Charles lost the war? Explain your answer.
On page 32 you chose to support either Charles or Parliament. Explain in your own words why you think your side won or lost the Civil War.

⟨◎⟩ Reactions to the Civil War

You have already seen in chapter three how the Civil War split the Verney family. The sources on these pages show how other people throughout the country felt about the war.

Source E

Certainly my affections to you are so unchangeable, that hostility itself cannot violate my friendship to your person. But I must be true to the cause wherein I serve. That great God which is the searcher of my heart knows with what a sad sense I go upon this service, and with what a perfect hatred I detest this war without an enemy; but I look upon it as *Opus Domini* [God's work], which is enough to silence all passion in me. The God of peace in his good time send us peace, and in the meantime fit us to receive it. We are both upon the stage, and must act those parts that are assigned us in this tragedy. Let us do it in a way of honour and without personal animosities.

(Extract from a letter from Sir William Waller, a Parliamentarian general, to his friend, the Royalist general, Sir Ralph Hopton)

Source F

Charlotte de la Tremouille, Countess of Derby.
During her husband's absence in the Isle of Man in 1644 she controlled large areas of Lancashire and Yorkshire for the Royalists, withstanding a siege of her home, Lathom House.

Source H

Having thus **possessed** themselves of the town they ran into every poor house cursing and damning, threatening and terrifying the poor women most terribly, setting naked swords and pistols to their breasts, they fell to plundering all the town before them. Picking purses and pockets, searching holes and corners, forcing people to deliver all the money they had. They beastly assaulted many women's chastity and impudently made brags of it afterwards. Nor did their rage here cease, but when the next day they were to march away from the town, they used all possible diligence in every street to kindle fire with gunpowder, match, wisps of straw, hay, burning coals etc. flung into any places where it was likely to catch hold.

(A Parliamentarian pamphlet, *Prince Rupert's Burning Love to England, discovered in Birmingham's flames*, 1643. Soldiers of both sides were guilty of looting captured towns)

Source I

The desires and Resolutions of the Clubmen of the counties of Dorset and Wiltshire: with articles of their covenant and certain directions for present behaviour, made and agreed at a meeting at Corehedge Corner on 25 May 1645, and read at Bradbury in Dorset by Mr Thomas Young, a lawyer; when there were present near 4,000 armed with clubs, swords, bills, pitchforks and other several weapons ... They will demand both sides to make peace; they will keep constant watch for any army, from either side, and defend themselves from them.

(Declaration of Clubmen, 1645. The clubmen were people who tried to prevent the armies of both sides entering their counties)

Source J

I had eleven horses taken away by the king's soldiers and four of the eleven were worth £40. The soldiers took the other nine away and I could never have them more. Since again going to market with a load of corn, the Earl of Manchester's soldiers [Parliamentary] met with my men and took away my whole team of horses. The king's soldiers call me Roundhead and the Parliament soldiers tell me I pay rent to Worcester [in Royalist hands].

(A Midland farmer)

Source G

Parliamentarian print showing the 'behaviour' of Royalist soldiers during the Civil War

The Souldiers in their passage to York turn unto reformers pull down Popish pictures, break down rayles, turn altars into Tables.

Source K

Royalist print showing Parliamentarian soldiers 'reforming' a church they did not approve of:

'The souldiers in their passage to York turn into reformers, pull down Popish pictures, break down rayles, turn altars into tables.'

Source L

We that had until then lived in great plenty and great order, found ourselves like fishes out of the water. For from as good a house as any gentleman in England had, we came to a baker's house in an obscure street, and from rooms well furnished, to be in a very bad bed in a garret, to one dish of meat, and that not the best ordered, not money, for we were as poor as Job, nor clothes more than a man or two brought in their cloak bags: we had the perpetual discourse [talk] of losing or gaining towns and men; at the windows the sad spectacle of war, sometimes plague, sometimes sickness of other kinds, by reason of so many people being packed together. I must needs say that most bore it with a martyr-like cheerfulness.

(Lady Fanshawe's Memoirs, written in 1665)

Source M

Catastrophic as the war could be for individual towns and agricultural areas, it may have been little worse than the natural hazards of fire, plague and harvest failure which were common to seventeenth-century society. It is possible that 100,000 people (out of a total population of about 5 million) were killed in the whole of the Civil War. This is about the same as the total deaths in London during 1665, the year of the Great Plague – and the visitations of plague in 1603 and 1625 had also been very severe. No single disaster in the Civil War could have been worse than the experience of a labouring man or woman who lived through the horrors of the Great Plague and then the inferno of the Great Fire.

(A modern historian putting the sufferings of the people during the Civil War in context)

John Lilburne (1615–1657) He was an officer in the Parliamentarian army and was best known as a leading figure among the Levellers. This radical political group was strong among the rank and file of the army in 1647–8.

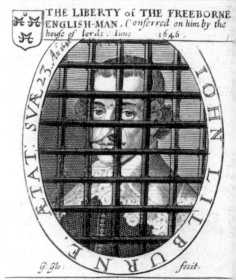

THE LIBERTY of THE FREEBORNE ENGLISH-MAN, *Conferred on him by the house of lords. Iune 1646.*

G: glo: *fecit.*

Gaze not upon this shaddow that is vaine,
But rather raise thy thoughts a higher straine,
To GOD (I meane) who set this young-man free,
And in like straits can eke deliuer thee.
Yea though the lords haue him in bonds againe,
LORD of lords will his iust cause maintaine.

The Levellers wanted Parliament to represent most of the people of England instead of just the landowners. The Levellers were stopped by the army commanders and Lilburne spent most of the rest of his life in prison.

EVIDENCE: REACTIONS TO THE CIVIL WAR

1. What evidence is there that some of those who took part in the Civil War regarded it as a tragedy?
2. Source H describes what happened when the Royalists captured Birmingham. What other source supports this account?
3. Sources G and H were produced by Parliamentarians to discredit the Royalists. Are they likely to be:
   a Accurate descriptions of what happened?
   b Exaggerated accounts of the events?
   c totally untrue?
   Explain your choice fully.
4. Which source might have been produced by Royalists to discredit the Parliamentarians?
5. What did the Clubmen (Source I) want? Use the sources to explain why movements like the Clubmen appeared as the war went on.
6. What do the sources tell you about the attitude of women to the Civil War?
7. You chose to support one of the sides. Why do you think many people tried to avoid being involved in the war?

◎ The execution of the king

At first MPs disagreed about whether to put Charles on trial. The majority believed that the only way to achieve peace was to continue negotiating with the king, even if that meant giving in to most of his demands. Other members felt that the king could not be trusted and had to be put on trial for starting the Second Civil War.

On 6 December 1648 the army sent Colonel Pride to prevent the supporters of negotiations entering Parliament: 231 members were either arrested or excluded from Parliament. The remaining 240 members were known as the Rump Parliament. On 1 January the Rump voted to put the king on trial.

The execution of Charles I, 30 January 1649. The Rump Parliament called him a 'tyrant, traitor and murderer, and a public and implacable enemy, to the Commonwealth of England'.

The charges against Charles

● As king of England he had been trusted to govern England according to the law.
● He had wickedly plotted to make himself a tyrant, ruling according to his will rather than according to the law.
● He had wickedly made war on his own subjects in his own interests and was therefore responsible for all the crimes committed in his name.
● He had asked for help against his own subjects from the French and the Dutch.
● He had restarted the war against Parliament and the people after being defeated.

Charles did not answer the charges. Instead he argued that the court had no right to try him. Charles said:

● He was the lawful king, responsible to God, and could not be brought to trial by his subjects.
● The law setting up the court had been made by the Commons alone. Neither the Lords nor the king had agreed to it. Therefore the court was not lawful.
● The real power behind the court was the army not the law or the rights of the people.

One hundred and thirty-five special judges, called commissioners, were appointed to try the king. In fact only eighty took part in the trial. Charles was found guilty by sixty-eight of the judges but only fifty-nine signed the death warrant.

PEOPLE IN THE PAST: THE KING'S TRIAL AND AFTER

1 Do you think Charles I was guilty of the charges against him? What evidence would you offer to support your answer?
2 Why do you think people disagreed about executing Charles?
3 Why do you think some of the judges did not sign the death warrant?
4 You chose to support either king or Parliament. Do you think Charles should have been executed? Give your reasons.

Cromwell and the crown

After the execution Parliament ruled England. Then in 1653 the army made Oliver Cromwell Lord Protector, with powers like those of a king. In 1657 Parliament asked Cromwell to take the title of king. Cromwell's contemporaries were divided as to whether or not he should accept the crown. You can read two opinions in sources N and O. Study them carefully, together with the points for and against acceptance. Then decide what you would have done if you had been Cromwell.

Source N

I am commanded by the Parliament of England, Scotland and Ireland to present this humble Petition and Advice unto your Highness. The first part of the body of government is the head. Parliament approved of the head but they liked not the name. They desire to give it a new name, which is of king, and hope that your Highness will take that name. It is a change of name only, and you are desired to take it by the agreement of all three nations in Parliament. The name and office of king is better known and more suitable to the laws and constitutions of these nations than that of a protector.

(Sir Thomas Widdrington's speech in the presence of Oliver Cromwell)

A contemporary drawing of Oliver Cromwell in his state robes as Lord Protector

Source O

I see that there are a number in Parliament that have voted kingship for you and that there are a small group there that are against it, and that the greatest part of the officers of the army are against it. I beg and beseech your Highness with tears and prayers to consider what you are doing. I have gone along with you since 1642. The experiences you have had of the power of God, methinks, should make you shrink from this threatening change.

(Letter from William Bradford, a former soldier, to Cromwell)

For

● Most people regarded kingship as the normal form of government for England.
● The existing form of government gave a lot more power to the army. This was very unpopular.
● If Cromwell became king there would be little chance of a restoration of the Stuarts.
● There would be fewer problems when Cromwell died because he could be succeeded as king by his son.

Against

● Most of Cromwell's supporters were in the army. They did not want him to become king.
● As king, Cromwell would have to accept the limitations on royal power in the laws of 1641.
● Cromwell had signed the death warrant of the last king of England, Charles I.
● There was little enthusiasm for a Stuart restoration in England. Cromwell already ruled England very much as a king would.

King Charles I sitting in state at the beginning of the Long Parliament (1640)

Oliver Cromwell's favourite daughter, Bettie, who died in 1658

Oliver Cromwell's oldest surviving son, Richard, who succeeded his father as Lord Protector in 1658 but resigned in May 1659

Oliver Cromwell: the man who refused to be king

Oliver Cromwell was the most important man in England for ten years. He became Parliament's most successful general and then ruled the country even though he refused to be king. At the time, people had very different opinions about Cromwell. Today people still disagree about him.

Oliver Cromwell was born in Huntingdon in 1599. His father was a country gentleman. He was educated at Huntingdon Grammar School and Cambridge University, where he was better known as a sportsman than as a student. He was first elected to Parliament as MP for Huntingdon in 1628.

During the Civil War, Cromwell's own regiment, the Ironsides, played an important part in winning the war. He then argued that Charles I had to be executed, but there is a story that he visited the king's coffin in secret and muttered 'Cruel necessity'.

After the execution, Parliament sent Cromwell to Ireland to put down a rebellion. He was successful, but the massacres at Drogheda and Wexford earned him a reputation for cruelty. In 1653 he was appointed Lord Protector with powers like those of a king.

Cromwell had strong religious views, but also encouraged religious toleration at a time when most people believed in imposing their religion on others. He used his powerful army and navy to fight a war against Spain. This made England a powerful country respected by her neighbours in Europe. However, many people in England thought of him as a military dictator.

Read the following views of Cromwell written by people who had met him.

Source P

In a word, as he had all the wickedness against which damnation is denounced, and for which hell-fire is prepared, so he had some virtues which have caused the memory of some men in all ages to be celebrated; and he will be looked upon by posterity as a brave bad man.

(Lord Clarendon, who supported Charles I and Charles II, although he also opposed some of Charles I's actions)

Source Q

Cromwell, our chief of men, who through a cloud
Not of war only, but detractions rude,
Guided by faith and matchless fortitude,
To peace and truth thy glorious way has ploughed.

(John Milton, the poet and Puritan, who was secretary to Cromwell's Council)

Source R

For to be Cromwell was a greater thing
Then aught below, or yet above, a king.

(Andrew Marvell, politician and poet, who supported Cromwell)

DIFFERENT VIEWS: OLIVER CROMWELL

Cromwell is often remembered as a wicked and evil man because he demanded Charles's execution.

1 Which source supports this view?
2 If you only had Sources Q and R what would you think of Cromwell?
3 Why do you think Milton and Marvell disagreed with Clarendon about Cromwell?
4 Do you agree with Clarendon that Cromwell was a brave bad man?
5 Compare your answer to question 4 with the answers of other people. Why do they agree or disagree?
6 Cromwell died in 1658. In 1660 England had a king again, Charles II. Think back to your choice of sides in the Civil War. Do you still think you were right to choose that side?

DAILY LIVES

Life in the Middle Ages had often been difficult and uncomfortable. Bad harvests and disease were always a danger. The greatest disaster was the Black Death, a plague that killed thirty per cent of people in the years from 1348. However, the people that survived became better off. Food was cheaper because there was plenty to spare. Workers could demand higher wages because there were not enough people to work in the fields. People in the 1400s had money to build larger houses, buy more clothes and food and pay for their children to go to school.

Perhaps the greatest change was that people were no longer villeins, having to work and live where their lords told them. The Black Death and Peasants' Revolt helped people win their freedom. Families who had been peasants were able to become rich landowners. The grandson of a merchant became a duke. A butcher's son, Thomas Wolsey, became Archbishop of York and Henry VIII's chief adviser.

This chapter's question for investigation is:

● **How did living standards change between 1500 and 1750?**

Before you look at the sources on pages 42–3 try to suggest answers

WILLIAM HARRISON'S LIST, 1577

The First Sort

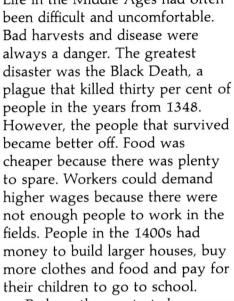

The Second Sort

Throughout the period 1500–1750 people knew which class they belonged to. William Harrison made a list of the classes in 1577 but people could change classes if they became richer or poorer.

The first sort:
lords and noblemen, bishops, knights, esquires and gentlemen.

The second sort:
citizens and burgesses – 'those that are free within the cities' – merchants.

The third sort:
yeomen 'freemen born English' – 'these commonly live wealthily, keep good houses and work to get riches. They are for the most part farmers'.

The fourth sort:
day labourers, poor farmers and all artificers such as tailors, shoemakers, carpenters, brickmakers, masons – 'they are to be ruled and not to rule others'.

The Third Sort

The Fourth Sort

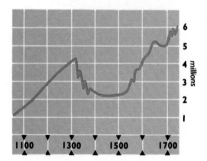

to the questions below, even if you are not sure about them. At the end of the chapter you will be asked questions 3 and 4 again. Then you will see how much you have learned.

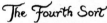

Changes in the total population from 1066–1750

DAILY LIVES: FIRST THOUGHTS

1   Make a list of the changes you would expect if living standards improved after 1500.

2   Look at the population graph. How do you think the changing population would affect the standard of living?

3   Do you think that living standards went up or down between 1500 and 1750?

4   What do you think might cause living standards to go up or down?

Living standards

The sources on these pages tell us about the daily lives of people between 1500 and 1750. What can you work out from the sources about how people's lives changed?

Source A

Gawsworth Hall, the home of a gentry family in the sixteenth century. The gentry were the wealthy landowners who lived very comfortably.

Source B

Ashdown House, the home of a gentleman's family in the eighteenth century

Source C

Examples of town fires

1585 Darlington – 273 houses burnt
1590 Wolverhampton – a five-day fire, little left untouched
1608 Bury St Edmunds – the town devastated
1628 Banbury – a third of the town destroyed
1653 Marlborough – 224 houses destroyed
1666 London – the Great Fire
1675 Northampton – the town destroyed
1688 Bungay – only one street untouched

Beccles in Suffolk had 4 large fires between 1500 and 1700

Source D

Examples of plagues

Worcester	1558, 1593–4, 1603, 1609, 1618, 1637, 1644–5
Leicester	1564, 1579, 1583, 1593, 1604, 1606–7, 1610–11, 1625–6, 1636, 1638–9
York	1604 – 30 per cent of people died
London	1665 – 70,000–100,000 died

Source E

In noblemen's houses it is not rare to see rich tapestries, silverware and other plate. Likewise in the houses of knights, gentlemen and merchants you can see tapestries, pewter, brass, fine linen and costly cupboards of plate. Many farmers also have beds with tapestries and silk hangings, tables with fine linen.

There are old men living in my village who say three things have altered marvellously in England within their memory: the multitude of chimneys lately erected, whereas in their younger days there were not above two or three in most towns; the great improvement of beds for we used to lie on straw sacks or rough mats; the exchange of vessels of wood into pewter and wooden spoons into silver or tin.

(William Harrison, *A Description of England*, 1577)

Source F

Things necessary for a dining room:

The room hung with pictures of all sorts, history, landscape, etc.
A large table, long, round or oval with falling leaves.
Side tables or cupboards for glasses and cups, spoons, sugar box and cruet for vinegar, oil and mustard pot.
Cistern of brass, pewter or lead to set flagons of beer and bottles of wine in.
Chairs and stools of Turkey work, Russia or calves leather or needlework.
Firegrate, fire shovel, tongs and irons all adorned with brass bobs and buttons.
Flowerpots or alabaster figures to adorn the windows and glass well-painted and a large seeing glass at the higher end of the room.

(A book of advice on furnishing, written in 1682 by Randle Holme, who was a close servant of Charles II)

Population

Real wage-rates

450   1500   1550   1600   1650   1700   1750

Source G

Changes in wages and the total population between 1450 and 1750

a What happened to wages when the population grew after 1500?
b Why did they increase from about 1650?

Source H

In the little parlour:
1 posted bedstead, 1 down bed, 2 pillows, 1 tapestry-covering with the curtains and furniture belonging to the same
3 back chairs with 5 buffet stools
7 glasses
1 warming pan and a little basket

In the great parlour:
1 great Bible and 35 other books
1 cupboard for the books and a desk where the Bible lies
1 framed table with 6 buffet stools, 5 low stools and 2 forms
1 pot with 5 pints of English honey
1 sugar box

In the great parlour chamber:
1 panelled bedstead, 1 feather bed, 3 pillows, 1 bolster, 1 flockbed, 2 blankets, 5 chests and 3 stools
28 pairs of fine jersey stockings
4 pillow cases, 13 table napkins, 1 hand towel and 2 table cloths
6 pairs of sheets and 1 odd sheet
1 embroidered nightcap
1 pair of silk garters and a ruff

In the buttery:
2 brass pots, 4 kettles, 2 skillets, a brass pan
2 brass candlesticks
17 pewter platters and dishes, 3 porringers, 5 saucers, 3 fruit dishes
Wooden dishes, spoons and trenchers
2 halberds, 1 pole-axe, 1 musket, 1 helmet

(Extracts from the 'true and perfect inventory' of Philip Cullyer of Wymondham, Norfolk, 1625)

Source I

There are in the town 2,207 people, of which 725 are not able to live without the charity of their neighbours. These are all begging poor. 100 householders who relieve others are but poor craftsmen. 160 householders are not able to relieve others. These are such as are not able to abide the storm of a fortnight's sickness but would be driven to beggary.

(A survey of the town of Sheffield, made in January 1615 by '24 of the most sufficient inhabitants')

Source J

Every woman is a sort of infant. It is seldom, almost never, that a married woman can have any action to use her wit only in her own name: her husband is her prime mover, without whom she cannot do much at home, and less abroad.

The husband is a priest unto his wife. He is the highest in the family and has authority over all. He is as a king in his house.

(Comments by men in the sixteenth century and in the 1620s)

Source K

It is a wife's duty to make a true reckoning and account to her husband of what she has received and what she had paid. And if her husband goes to market to buy or sell, as they often do, he should show his wife in like manner. For if one of them should try to deceive they will not thrive and therefore must be true to each other.

(Sir Anthony Fitzherbert, *Book of Husbandry*, 1523)

Source L

A woman soldier in the seventeenth century. This illustration is from a ballad telling of a girl who became a drummer boy in the Civil War and was successful in her disguise until she had a baby!

✻ Living standards – some conclusions

Source M

This chart shows how the weather never regained the warmth of the period between 1100 and 1300. Cold, wet winters became more common during the years 1500–1700.

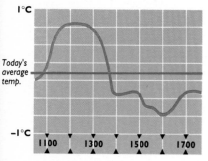

Difficult roads helped to make travelling very slow compared with today as you can see from this map. The numbers after each town name represent the number of hours journey time from London in 1750 by the fastest coach.

However, people were travelling in a little more comfort and travelling more often. The rich travelled to London to the king's court and to fashionable places like Bath to show off their wealth and importance.

In the 1500s and 1600s life had not changed much from the Middle Ages. There were still the dangers of plagues and poor harvests. People suffered and could do little to help themselves apart from wait for better times. Some years were far worse than others. For example, in the late 1540s prices were rising quickly, partly because of the huge costs of Henry VIII's wars. On top of this came disastrous harvests and people simply starved – there were stories of people eating acorns. Then influenza killed twenty per cent of the population between 1555 and 1560. Rising prices made life very difficult for the poor. Prices went up eightfold between 1500 and 1640 but wages only rose threefold. People on low wages suffered badly.

But many people's lives were becoming more comfortable. In larger houses there was far more good furniture. In 1500 most houses had three rooms, but in the 'housing revolution' of 1570 to 1610 many new houses were built with four or five rooms, and by 1650 many had six or more rooms. This meant people had more privacy and different rooms for eating and entertaining.

Improvements in agriculture, increased trade and more navigable rivers were helping to make England prosperous. Trade also gave people a more varied diet. Coffee and tea began to replace ale as the main drink. Potatoes were imported and became common by 1700. Less healthy was the increased use of sugar and the arrival of tobacco. People still preferred plenty of meat because it was the food of the rich. Vegetables remained the food of the poor.

The 1400s had been a good time for women who wanted to work for themselves. The population was low so there was enough work for both men and women. As the population rose again, women found it more and more difficult to become apprentices or have their own businesses. Men protected themselves by arguing that the Bible said that men were superior.

Edinburgh 230
Newcastle 132
Leeds 84
Liverpool 84
Manchester 80
Sheffield 60
Shrewsbury 75
Birmingham 36
Norwich 36
Bristol 40
Bath 36
London
Exeter 40
Dover 27

☐ 1 day's journey from London
☐ 2 day's journey from London

EVIDENCE: LIVING STANDARDS 1500–1750

1 How useful for your investigation of daily life are Sources A, F, and I?
2 How useful for your investigation of daily life are Sources A, H, and I?
3 How useful for your investigation are Sources E and G? investigation?
4 Many foreign visitors commented that England was a very rich country. What questions would you want to ask before you decided whether they were reliable accounts?
5 There were two queens of England in the 1500s. Does this prove that women had more rights after 1500?
6 Do you think that living standards improved or fell after 1500?

❇ New ideas

Another sign of improvement was that people had more spare time. The richer people became, the more time they had to take advantage of the changes that came after the Renaissance.

The Renaissance was a revival or 'rebirth' of learning which began in Italy and then spread north. It was called a rebirth because people felt they were rediscovering Greek and Roman ideas about art, science and philosophy. However, it was more than just a rediscovery. New ideas developed and new discoveries were made.

● *Did the Renaissance lead to an improvement in science and education in England? Did people treat each other better because of these new ideas?*

What can you discover from the sources on pages 45–49?

Education

Source A

We found a shepherd and his little boy reading, far from any houses or sight of people, the Bible.

(Samuel Pepys, *Diary*, 14 July 1667)

Source B

The Bible in English under every weaver's and chambermaid's arms hath done us much hurt. Universities abound with too many scholars. That which hath done us most harm is the abundance of grammar schools. There are so many schools now as most read. So there should be but such a proportion as to serve the church and, moderately, the law and the merchants. The rest for labour, for else they run to idle people. When most was unlettered it was much a better world both for peace and war.

(The Duke of Newcastle's advice to Charles II, 1660)

Source C

About 5 years old, I was put to school, but being addicted to play I scarcely learnt to distinguish my letters before I was taken away to work for my living. About 13 years old I could not read, then thinking of the vast usefulness of reading I bought me a primer, and got now one, and then another, to teach me to spell, and so learned to read imperfectly. But in a little time I was desirous to learn to write but none of my fellow-shepherds being able to teach me. I bethought myself of a lame young man who taught some poor people's children to read and write and agreed with him to give him one of my sheep to teach me to make the letters, and Join them together.

(*Memoirs of the Life of Thomas Tryon*, a London merchant, 1705)

Source D
A picture of Oliver Cromwell's teacher

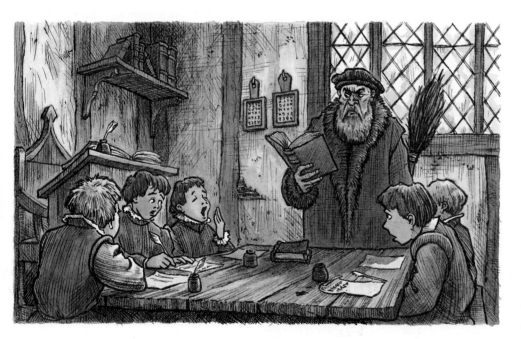

Source E

William Harvey (1578–1657)
He was the first person to describe accurately the way blood circulates around the body. This picture shows part of Harvey's work but it was many years before most doctors believed his ideas.

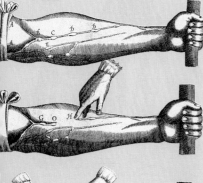

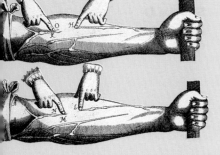

Source I

Sir Isaac Newton (1642–1727)
He was a great scientist and invented a new kind of telescope that is the basis for many telescopes today, but his most important ideas were about gravity and the movements of the earth, the moon and the planets.

New science – new attitudes?

Source F

Mr Hobbes used to say that he had rather have the advice or take medicine from an experienced old woman, that had been at many sick people's bed-sides, than from the learnedest but unexperienced physician.

(John Aubrey, *Brief Lives*, written around 1680. Thomas Hobbes was a famous philosopher)

Source G

To cure quartans [malaria] and the gout, take the hair and nails of the patient, cut them small and either give them to the birds in a roasted egg, or put them in a hole in an oak tree or a plane tree. Stop up the hole with a peg of the same tree.

(*The New London Dispensary*, a book of remedies produced in 1682)

Source H

2 Feb. 1685. His Majesty was walking about when he felt some unusual disturbance in his brain, followed by loss of speech and convulsions. The king's physicians opened a vein in his right arm and drew off about 16 ounces of blood. To free his stomach of all impurities they administered an emetic [to make him vomit]. Soon after they gave [laxative] pills to drain away the humours. Blistering agents were applied all over his head, after his hair had been shaved.
4 Feb. The Physicians administered: Spirit of human skull 40 drops, taken in an ounce and a half of Cordial julep.
6 Feb. The King died soon after noon.

(An account of Charles II's death by his chief physician)

Source J

I went to see the Barbers Surgeon Hall in Newcastle. There I saw a room with a round table in it, railed around with seats for convenience in their dissecting and anatomising a body and reading lectures on all parts. Two bodies had been anatomised. One the bones were fastened with wires, the other had had the flesh boiled off. The ligaments remained and the parts were held together by its own muscles and sinews.

(*The Journal of Celia Fiennes*, 1698)

Source K

Lord! to see how much of my old folly and childishness hangs upon me still that I cannot forbear carrying my watch in my hand in the coach all this afternoon, and seeing what o'clock it is one hundred times, and am apt to think with myself, how could I be so long without one.

(Samuel Pepys, *Diary*, 13 May 1665)

Source L

Robert Boyle. His great delight is chemistry. He has at his sister's a noble laboratory and several servants (apprentices to him) to look after it. He is charitable to ingenious men that are in want and foreign chemists have had large proof of his bounty, for he will not spare for cost to get any rare secret.

(John Aubrey, *Brief Lives*, written around 1680. Boyle was one of the leading scientists in the 1600s and a member of the Royal Society)

Source M

The design of the Royal Society is to make faithful records of all the works of nature and art so that the present age may mark errors and restore truths. The business of their weekly meetings is to account Philosophical Experiments and Observations, to consider how they may be improved for the benefit of mankind. They have made enquiries into eclipses, comets, meteors, plants, animals, earthquakes, tides, currents and many hundreds of things.

(E. Chamberlayne, *The Present State of England*, 1687. Charles II became patron of the Royal Society in 1662)

Source N

To Gresham College where Mr Hooke read a very curious lecture about the late comet, among other things proving very probably that this is the very same comet that appeared before in 1618 and that in such a time it will probably appear again – which is a very new opinion – but all will be in print.

(Samuel Pepys, *Diary*, 1 March 1665. Pepys was describing a meeting of the Royal Society)

Source O

There was great interest in geography and exploration. One geographer, Richard Hakluyt, collected and published accounts of voyages to distant parts of the world. This picture shows Willem Barents' search for the North West passage.

Source P

If she swim, take her up, and cause some women to search her. If they find any extraordinary marks about her, let her be bound a second time with her right thumb bound to her left toe and her left thumb to her right toe. Your men have the rope to preserve her and then throw her into the water. If she swim she is a witch. I have seen it often tried in the north parts.

(A seventeenth-century account of how to identify witches)

Source Q

John Lowes had been a vicar here about 50 years. He was executed at St Edmondsbury with 60 more for being a wizard. Hopkins, his chief accuser, kept the old man waking miserably several nights until he was delirious. The truth is he made his parishioners uneasy and they were glad to take advantage of those wicked times and get him hanged.

(An entry in a church register, written after 1660)

Source R

The poor and impotent persons of every parish shall be relieved [helped]. Every person will of their charity give weekly. The relief shall be gathered by collectors and weekly distributed to the poor.

(From the Poor Law Act of 1601)

Source S

In the ten weeks between 6 October 1590 and 14 December, 71 persons, male or female, and aged 14 upwards, were sentenced to be severely whipped and branded with a hot iron for being masterless vagrants in the county.

(Middlesex County Records)

Source U

Bulls and bears are fastened behind and then are worried by great English bulldogs. It sometimes happens that the dogs are killed on the spot; fresh ones are immediately supplied. To this entertainment there follows the whipping of a blinded bear by 5 or 6 men. He defends himself with all his force and skill, tearing the whips out of their hands.

(A sixteenth-century account by a German visitor to England)

Source T

Immigrants from far away began to come to Britain but many were unwilling visitors. Explorers brought back 'Indians' from America and the first slaves arrived from Africa.

Source V

Hanging – the punishment for persistent vagrants (homeless wanderers and beggars) who had already been branded for their first offence

A

B

C

D

Art

Picture B is a portrait of Henry VI. This was the kind of painting done in England in the early 1500s. Look at the other pictures.

- How does this compare with the work of European painters in the 1500s?
- How did artists' skills develop in the next 200 years?

A Anne of Cleves by Hans Holbein, mid-1500s
C Ippolito de'Medici and Mario Bracci by Girolamo, early 1500s
D The Tichborne Dole by Gillis van Tilborg, late 1600s
E The artist's daughters by Thomas Gainsborough, mid-1700s

E

New ideas: some conclusions

Between 1500 and 1750 many more schools were started. People realised the importance of being able to read and write but, again, this was a development that had begun in the 1400s and now continued even more quickly. Girls were not as well educated as boys. Men believed women were inferior, educating them was a waste of time and might even be dangerous!

Many people had a wide range of interests – science, geography, exploration and even history! Scientific ideas helped to stop the hunt for witches later in the seventeenth century. Scientific discoveries also paved the way for the great industrial revolution of the next century and more medical developments. Even so, there was much still to learn and many things were half-understood. Doctors were still helpless when there were epidemics.

Renaissance ideas about art also reached Britain but Britain did not produce any great artists until the 1700s. Music, theatre and writing were different. Unfortunately, we cannot give a free cassette with this book so you will have to find for yourself the beautiful music by Byrd, Tallis, Gibbons or Purcell. You will have heard of at least one book from this time – *Robinson Crusoe* by Daniel Defoe. Theatre was popular with all groups, rich and poor. Although Shakespeare's plays can be difficult for us to understand, people went to listen to the jokes and to see the French beaten in *Henry V* as well as to follow the tragic and exciting plots.

Blood sports, such as cock-fighting, remained popular entertainments in the 1700s. Why not, when people were used to seeing human beings die or be branded as punishments? Bare-fist boxing in the 1700s was only slightly less bloody. The development of horse-racing and cricket at rich country houses was quieter but there was heavy gambling at these events as well.

A firework display on the River Thames in 1749 paid for by the Duke of Richmond. The music was provided by George Handel who spent much of his life in England.

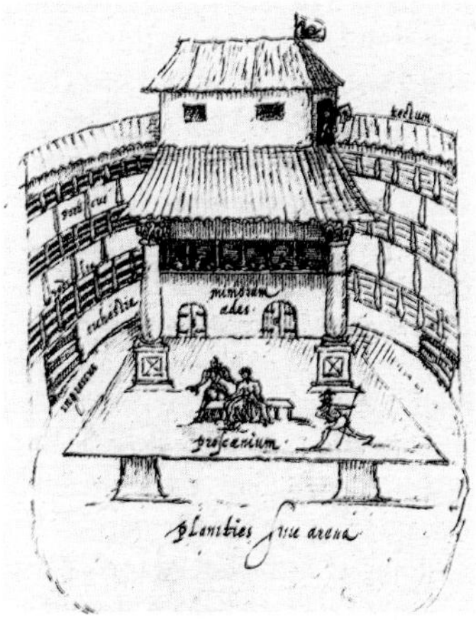

The first theatres were built in the late 1500s. Audiences were varied: the rich sat to watch the plays but others stood. Actors and writers could earn their living but there were no actresses, as boys played female roles until the late seventeenth century.

EVIDENCE: NEW IDEAS 1500–1750

1. How useful for your investigation are Sources B and Q?
2. How useful for your investigation are Sources L and U?
3. How useful are Sources R, S and V for finding out about attitudes to the poor?
4. How reliable are Sources F, G and H as evidence of medical treatment?
5. Is Source M more or less reliable than Source N as evidence for the work of the Royal Society?
6. Does the evidence on pages 45–9 support or change your ideas about the standard of living after 1500?

A sixteenth-century picture of King Arthur. People enjoyed the stories of King Arthur and the Round Table. Arthur was often drawn as a knight in armour even though the stories were about a time one thousand years before such armour was used.

Stonehenge was a great puzzle but many people thought they knew the answer. Some said that it was a Roman temple. Others said that it was the place where the Vikings chose their kings. In the 1740s William Stukeley had a different idea. He said that Stonehenge was a temple where the Druids worshipped their gods and killed people as sacrifices. This picture shows the kinds of scenes Stukeley imagined. What he did not know was that the last building at Stonehenge took place a thousand years before the time of the Druids.

※ Interested in history?

Yes, people were interested in history! More people could read history books. People were proud of their country and wanted to know more about its past. People also thought the study of history was useful, good training for government officials. In 1582 the Queen's Council wanted a new history of England to be written for schools – in Latin verse! It was to be 'heroical and of good instruction'. Others thought history was dangerous. James I tried to ban Raleigh's *History of the World* because it was 'saucy about princes'.

At first historians did not have many sources to use. After the Dissolution of the Monasteries, documents had been scattered – even used to wrap fish! In the 1600s many documents were collected, copied and printed so that more people could read and learn from them. Historians' skills were developing. They were using more sources. Their explanations for events were careful and complex. They were beginning to understand that the past was different from their own time, but they still misunderstood the past as you can see in the examples on this page.

King John: two interpretations

The sixteenth-century story

John was a good king because he stood up for England and his own rights as king against the Pope. He stopped the Pope interfering in England and then had to fight off a foreign invasion. There were also plots against him, involving his cousin Arthur who had to be executed. Magna Carta was not mentioned in Shakespeare's play about John.

The seventeenth-century story

John demanded too many taxes and did not take the advice of his barons. This led to civil war. The barons rebelled to reduce John's power but he had to be beaten in war before he agreed to Magna Carta, a new set of rules for governing the country.

DIFFERENT VIEWS: UNDERSTANDING HISTORY

1 Why did people in the sixteenth century think John was a good king? (It will help you if you think about what happened in the sixteenth century.)
2 Why did ideas about John change in the seventeenth century?
3 What is an anachronism?
4 Explain one anachronism from this page.
5 Did people in the sixteenth and seventeenth centuries think the past was just the same as their own times?

✳ People in the past

The people you have been investigating wore different clothes, lived in different kinds of houses and even had different accents to yours. It is easy to think that they were completely different from us, but were they? Here are some sources written by real, individual people. Are they completely different from us or very like us?

Source A

Myself somewhat vexed at my wife's neglect in leaving of her scarf, waistcoat and night-dressings in the coach today that brought us from Westminster, though I confess she did give them to me to look after – yet it was her fault not to see that I did take them out of the coach.

(Samuel Pepys, *Diary*, 6 January 1663)

Source B

Glory to God we never had but one mind throughout our lives, our souls were wrapped up in each other, our aims and designs one, our loves one and our resentments one. We so studied one the other that we knew each other's mind by our looks; whatever was real happiness, God gave it me in him.

(Lady Fanshawe (1625–80) writing about her husband)

Source C

I was gone to Chester when he died, my business being urgent, and he in a hopeful way of recovery when I set out. Being there I had an irresistible impression upon my spirit that I must need go home that night and went home, where I found a sad and dis-tracted family that needed much consola-tion. I do verily believe that strong impression was from some angel that God employed to help that work.

(Adam Martindale's diary, 23 August 1659, recording the death of his eight-year-old son)

Source D

If they see a foreigner very well made, or particularly handsome, they will say, it is a pity he is not an Englishman.

(A German traveller's comment on the English in 1598)

Source E

You would never believe how friendly our people are together and the English are the same and quite loving to our people. If you come here with half your property you would never think of going back to Flanders. Send my money and the three children. Come at once and do not be anxious.

(A letter by Clais van Wervekin to his wife in 1567. He was a religious refugee who found work in Norwich)

Source F

The people, nothing rejoicing, held down their heads sorrowfully. As the Spanish ambassador rode through London the boys pelted him with snowballs. When they heard the news of the marriage treaty the people very much misliked it, each man was abashed.

(The English reaction to Queen Mary's marriage to Philip of Spain in 1554, described in the *Chronicle of Queen Jane and Queen Mary*, written in the 1550s)

Source G

Lord Cobham and his family in 1567. What can you work out about ideas and attitudes from this picture?

❊ A country of differences?

In 1750 most people still lived by farming, just as they always had done. However, there were many changes. Towns were growing, trade was increasing and, as you have seen, standards of living were improving for many people. Yet life was not the same for everyone. The rich had very much more comfortable lives than the yeomen – the middling sort – but the yeomen were also far better off than the wage labourers. There were many differences across the country too.

Source I

The whole kingdom, the people, the land and even the sea are employed to furnish something, and I may add, the best of everything, to supply the city of London with provisions; I mean by provisions, corn, flesh, fish, butter, cheese, salt, fuel, timber, etc. and cloths also; with everything necessary for building.

(Daniel Defoe, *A Tour through the Whole Island of Great Britain*, 1724–6)

Source H

The country's largest towns in 1400 and 1700. What changes can you see? Is there a pattern to the changes?

Town populations in 1400
- over 10 000   △ 3000–5000
- 5000–10 000

Town populations in 1700
- over 10 000
- 5000–10 000

Source J

Liverpool is built just on the Mersey, mostly new-built houses of brick and stone after the London fashion. The first original [town] was a few fishermen's houses and now is grown to a large fine town of 24 streets; there is indeed a little chapel and there are a great many dissenters in the streets. There are abundance of persons very well dressed and of good fashion. The streets are fair and long. It's London in miniature as much as ever I saw anything.

Leeds is a large town, several large streets, clean and good houses all built of stone. Some have good gardens and steps up to their houses. This is esteemed the wealthiest town of its bigness in the country, its manufacture is the woollen cloth in which they are all employed. This town is full of dissenters, there are two large meeting places and also a good school for young gentlewomen. The streets are very broad, the market large.

At **Gloucester** they follow knitting, stockings, gloves, waistcoats and petticoats and sleeves all of cotton and others spin the cotton.

Nottingham is the neatest town I have seen. They make brick and tile by the town. The manufacture of the town mostly consists of weaving of stockings which is a very ingenious art. There was a man there that spun glass and made several things in glass,

1 Which areas of the country were the richest and the poorest in 1688?
2 Which kinds of towns were becoming larger and more important?
3 Which kinds of towns were becoming less important?
4 Why do you think some areas were richer than others?
5 How important was London for the rest of the country?
6 How does Celia Fiennes's evidence support the idea that there were many differences in the way people lived around the country?
7 There were many changes in the standard of living. Were these changes always improvements? Explain your answer.

Source K
Industries in Britain around 1700.

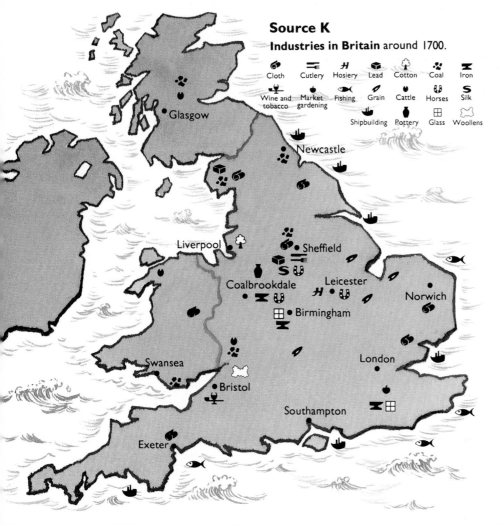

Cloth · Cutlery · Hosiery · Lead · Cotton · Coal · Iron · Wine and tobacco · Market gardening · Fishing · Grain · Cattle · Horses · Silk · Shipbuilding · Pottery · Glass · Woollens

Glasgow · Newcastle · Liverpool · Sheffield · Coalbrookdale · Leicester · Norwich · Birmingham · Swansea · London · Bristol · Southampton · Exeter

Land tax for counties in 1692
over £2 per house
£1.50–£2 per house
under £1.50 per house

Source L

Were some areas richer than others? This map shows the amount of land tax paid for houses in 1692.

birds and beasts. With coloured glass he makes buttons which are very strong and will not break. Nottingham is famous for good ale.

As I drew nearer and nearer to **Newcastle [upon Tyne]** I met with and saw an abundance of little carriages with a yoke of oxen and a pair of horses together, which are to convey the coal from the pits to the barges on the river. The country all about is full of this coal. The sulphur of it taints the air and it smells strongly to strangers. Upon a high hill two miles from Newcastle I could see all about the country which was full of coal pits.

In most parts of **Somerset** it is very fruitful for orchards, plenty of apples and pears, but they are not curious in planting the best sort of fruit, which is a great pity; being so soon produced, and such quantities, they are likewise as careless when they make cider. They press all sorts of apples together, else they would have a good cider as any other parts, even as good as Hertfordshire.

(Extracts from the *Journal of Celia Fiennes*, who lived from 1662 to 1741. She was a very independent woman and between 1685 and 1710 she explored England, writing down her comments on what she saw. She travelled on horseback, sometimes with only a couple of servants for company. Her father had been a colonel in Cromwell's army and Celia, too, was a dissenter in religion)

By 1750 newspapers had become so common that they were taxed and were therefore too expensive for ordinary people to buy. Kings and governments also censored the newspapers, so they were not free to print what they wished. Even so, newspapers helped news to spread more quickly. This picture shows a lady selling the London Gazette.

※ The causes of change

Between 1500 and 1750, people in Britain became much more prosperous. However, some people did better than others. There were great differences, depending upon the kind of work that people did or the region they lived in. Men continued to have far more freedom than women, although some women, like Celia Fiennes, did not do what men expected. Why did these changes happen?

The development of printing spread ideas more quickly.

Many people were richer and better educated.

Causes of change

People wanted to live more comfortably.

The population gradually increased.

There was more trade at home and more goods came from abroad.

Source M
Of Marriage and Populacy. The country complains of small trade of commodities, which proceeds especially from want of people. If we have but a million more people than now we should quickly see how trade would alter for the better.

(Carew Reynell, *The True English Interest*, 1674)

Source N
Nothing has wrought such an alteration in the order of the people as the introduction of trade. This has given a new face to the whole nation and has almost totally changed the manners, customs and habits of the people, more especially the lower sort. The narrowness of their future is changed into wealth.

(Henry Fielding, *Enquiry into the causes of the late increase in robbers*, 1750)

CAUSES AND CONSEQUENCES: WHY DID DAILY LIFE IMPROVE?

1 Explain how each cause in the diagram helped to change the way people lived.
2 Which reason or reasons do you think were the most important?
3 How did changes in the number of people affect trade?
4 How did changes in communications affect trade?
5 Explain in your own words:
   a how living standards changed between 1500 and 1750
   b why living standards changed between 1500 and 1750

A UNITED KINGDOM?

In 1690 the armies of ex-King James II of England and of King William III of England fought a battle on the banks of the River Boyne in Ireland.

James had been deposed as king in 1688 because the Protestant majority in England was afraid that he would try to make England into a Catholic country and rule without Parliament. The English lords had invited James's son-in-law, William Prince of Orange, a Dutch Protestant, to become king in his place.

James's supporters were known as Jacobites (the Latin for James is Jacobus). In Scotland the Jacobites were only a minority and were soon defeated. In Ireland almost all the Catholics and even many Protestants supported James. They joined his army to fight William.

At the Battle of the Boyne, William III's army was victorious. James fled to France. He had lost all his three kingdoms, but support for James, and later for his son, did remain strong in Scotland and Ireland. England's conflict with France also continued and the French tried to weaken England by helping the Jacobites. As a result of this the English wanted to strengthen their control over Scotland and Ireland.

In this chapter we shall see how and why England, Ireland, Scotland and Wales moved towards being one country. The main question you will be investigating will be:

- *Did England, Scotland, Wales and Ireland become more united between 1500 and 1750?*

The Battle of the Boyne

Source A

That Ireland is a distinct realm.

How can the Irish at all be truly deemed rebels to the Prince of Orange, by rising for King James the second against the said Prince, created king by the people of England? Was not James the second acknowledged the lawful king of the three kingdoms and as such did he not reign four years? What should then oblige the people of Ireland to disown him, their lawful sovereign, for the rest of his life? But you'll say that England, the principal kingdom of the monarchy, ought to be followed by Ireland in owning or disowning the kings of that monarchy. We answer thus: the behaviour herein of the people of England is no rule to Ireland, a distinct realm, a different nation, having different laws and a Parliament of her own.

(A Jacobite narrative of the war in Ireland)

The kingdoms of Britain 1066-1500

In 1500 the British Isles were made up of four countries.

Scotland was an independent kingdom, often at war with England. English kings had claimed rights over the Scottish kings but these claims had been vigorously resisted. In order to preserve its independence, Scotland had frequently allied with England's enemy, France.

English kings found it difficult to control the **northern counties** of their own country. William the Conqueror had smashed resistance in the North shortly after he became king but there was always a possibility that powerful northern lords would act independently. This part of the country was governed through a special Council of the North.

English kings had claimed the right to rule **Ireland**. Some English lords had gone to Ireland and established control over certain parts of the island. The Anglo-Irish lords accepted that the king of England was their overlord, but in practice English control over Ireland was only really effective in the area around Dublin.

The English had conquered **Wales** in the thirteenth century, ending the rule of native princes. From that time on the eldest son of the English monarch has been called the Prince of Wales. The Welsh never completely accepted the conquest and there was a serious Welsh rising under Owain Glyndwr in the early fifteenth century. Wales was run separately from England, through a Council of Wales and the Marches (borders).

1750 – a united kingdom?

By 1750 many changes had taken place. England had been ruled by Scottish kings and later by German kings. England and Wales had become one country with the same Parliament and laws. England and Scotland had been united and their parliaments had merged. The English had conquered Ireland but had left it as a separate country, controlled by England.

Copy the chart below to keep a record of your findings about the making of the United Kingdom.

They could merge together completely so that they had the same Government, the same laws and the same religion.

They could have the same king but each have its own Government, Parliament, laws and religion.

There were several forms into which two countries could be united:

They could have the same Government and Parliament but have different laws and religion.

	Kind of union achieved	By agreement or force?
Wales		
Scotland		
Ireland		

How was a kingdom united?

It could be united by:
- agreement
- force
- the king of one country inheriting the throne of another country.

Wales

During the Middle Ages there had been a lot of fighting between the English and the Welsh. The Welsh had struggled unsuccessfully to stop the English from taking over their country. When Henry Tudor, the grandson of a Welshman, became King Henry VII of England, the Welsh people were pleased. They looked on the Tudors as Welsh and the Tudor monarchs encouraged this idea because it helped to make their laws more popular in Wales.

Henry VIII decided that England and Wales should have one system of government and one set of laws. The Acts of Union of 1536 and 1542 divided Wales into counties like the English ones, English law was used in Wales and Welsh members were elected to the Parliament in Westminster. The Welsh did not object to these things for three reasons. Firstly, they were done by a 'Welsh' king so there was no offence to their national pride. Secondly, the union brought better trade with England which made the Welsh gentry better off. Thirdly, they had no choice.

Crown Lands

Anglesey
Caernarfon
Denbigh
Flint
Mérioneth
Montgomery
Cardigan Bay
Cardigan
Radnor
Pembroke
Carmarthen
Brecon
Glamorgan
Monmouth
England

Map of Wales showing the new counties set up under Henry VIII

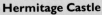 Scotland

Scotland had always allied with France for protection against the English. This friendship was known as the 'Auld Alliance'. It meant that any conflict between England and France was likely to involve Scotland. Scotland and France fought many wars against England between 1300 and 1560.

The area which suffered most was the Borders. Armies fought across it, the crops were burned, the people were robbed and killed on both sides. Local people stole each other's cattle and killed each other in long-running feuds. The wars continued even when the countries were supposed to be at peace. Governments were reluctant to punish their own citizens for making war on the enemy.

Hermitage Castle
This grim fortress was one of the many castles built along both sides of the border. They were both places to retreat to when under attack and bases from which to launch raids on their neighbours across the border.

Mary Queen of Scots

Henry VII of England wanted peace. He avoided war with France and married his daughter Margaret to King James IV of Scotland. Henry VIII was more aggressive and there was war with Scotland in 1513. Then in the 1540s Henry wanted his five-year-old son to marry the infant Mary Queen of Scots. Henry thought this would end the threat from the North. However he sent an army to make the marriage happen. The Scots took fright and in 1548 they sent the five-year-old Mary to France. Ten years later she married the French king's eldest son. These wars did England little good.

While Mary Queen of Scots was in France, Scotland was ruled by her French mother. Elizabeth I helped the Scottish Protestants to seize control of the country and drive out the French. Mary returned to Scotland in 1561 but in 1568 she quarrelled with the Protestant Scottish lords. She was driven out and her infant son James was made king. She fled to England where at first Elizabeth kept her a prisoner. In 1587 Mary was executed.

After Mary's death her son, King James VI, a Protestant, became Elizabeth's heir. When she died he became king of England.

Mary claimed she had a better right to the English throne than Elizabeth I because she was a Catholic. When Mary's first husband became king of France, she was called queen of France, Scotland, and England. Her coat of arms included the royal badges of all three countries.

The Union of the Crowns

When James VI of Scotland became James I of England he was king of two separate countries. Each country had its own laws, its own different Protestant Church, its own Parliament and its own money. The only thing they had in common was the king. James chose to live in England because it was the richer and more powerful of the two countries.

The Union of the Crowns did bring benefits. There was a quick end to the troubles in the Borders. England no longer needed to fear that enemy countries would ally with Scotland and threaten her from the north.

Source B

I am the Husband and the whole Isle is my lawful Wife; I am the head; and it is my Body; I am the Shepherd and it is my flock; I hope therefore that no man will be so unreasonable as to think that I who am a Christian King under the Gospel should be husband to two wives; that I being the head should have a divided and monstrous body.

(Speech of James I to his first English Parliament, March 1604)

Source C

One man is owner of two pastures, with one hedge to divide them; the one pasture bare, the other fertile and good: a wise owner will not pull down the hedge but make gates to let them in and out, otherwise the cattle will rush in and not want to return.

(Nicholas Fuller MP, arguing in Parliament against union in 1607)

Source D

As for embodying Scotland with England it will be as when the poor bird is embodied into the hawk that hath eaten it up.

(Reverend Robert Blair)

James VI & I was king of England as well as king of Scotland. The picture on the left shows James when he was king of Scotland and the picture on the right shows him after he became king of England.

THE UNION OF THE CROWNS

1 Why do you think England and Scotland were so often at war with each other?

2 What does Hermitage Castle tell you about life in the Borders?

3 'The marriage of Margaret Tudor and James IV brought England and Scotland closer together.' How true do you think this was:
   a in the 1540s?   b in the 1560s?
   c in 1603?

4 What advantages did England gain from the Union of the Crowns?

5 What advantages did Scotland gain from the Union of the Crowns?

6 James I and Charles I wanted England and Scotland to become one country. Why do you think they wanted this?

7 Why did other English and Scottish people want their countries to remain separate?

Source E

We noblemen, gentlemen, and citizens in the kingdoms of England, Scotland and Ireland, by the providence of God living under one king, and being of one reformed religion [are] determined to enter into a mutual and solemn league and covenant, to which we all agree and swear:

1 We shall try to bring the churches of God in the three kingdoms to having the same beliefs and religious practice.

3 We shall try to preserve the rights and privileges of Parliaments, the liberties of the kingdoms and the King's Majestic person and authority.

5 And because peace between these kingdoms was denied in former times to our ancestors, we shall all endeavour that they may remain joined in a firm peace and union for ever.

(Solemn League and Covenant, 1643)

The road to Union

Most Scots helped Parliament in the Civil War against Charles I because they had similar religious ideas. They made an agreement called the Solemn League and Covenant to work towards a single Church for all of Britain.

However, the trial and execution of their king by the English came as a great shock to many Scots. The English Parliament also overturned the religious agreement. The Scots promptly recognised Charles II as their king.

Oliver Cromwell could not allow Scotland to be used as a base for attacks on England. He attacked and defeated the Scots. The Scottish Parliament was abolished and forty Scottish Members joined the four hundred English Members of the Westminster Parliament.

At the Restoration, Charles II restored the Scottish Parliament but made sure that it had very little power.

After 1688 the Scots were divided. Some supported William III but others wanted independence. When George I became king of England some Scots wanted a Stuart king. This would have meant an end to the Union of the Crowns. It might also have started a new alliance between France and Scotland. The English were prepared to offer the Scots generous terms for a full union. In 1707 the English and Scottish Parliaments voted to merge and England and Scotland became one country.

There was no guarantee that the union would last. Riots in the Scottish towns showed how unpopular it was with many ordinary people. Many Highlanders saw little benefit to them in union and supported rebellions in favour of the Stuarts in 1708, 1715 and 1745. The English went back on their promises to the Scots at the time of the union and in 1713 the Scottish MPs at Westminster tried to repeal the Act of Union.

The advantages and disadvantages of Union

Advantages
● Scotland was a very poor country and would be better off joined with much richer England.
● Scotland could trade with the English empire, including North America.
● Most Scots were Protestants and did not want a Catholic king. They preferred Protestant George I to Catholic James.
● James's supporters were mostly highlanders. The majority of Scotsmen were lowlanders who looked on the highlanders as savages and thieves. Union with England might bring law and civilisation to the highlands.

Disadvantages
● Some Scottish industries would suffer from competition with more successful English ones.
● There might be less trade with France.
● English Protestantism was very different from Scottish Protestantism. Scots feared English interference in their church.
● Scotland would lose her identity and independence. She would be swallowed up by the richer and more powerful England.

PEOPLE IN THE PAST: THE ACT OF UNION 1707

1 The English opposed union with Scotland even when James I came to the throne. Why did they change their minds after 1700?
2 How do you think the following people would have felt about union with England? Take into account the list of advantages and disadvantages.

a A Glasgow merchant interested in developing the tobacco trade with America.
b A Highland chief, educated in France and a strong Catholic.
c A minister of the Church of Scotland.

The last revolt

On 25 July 1745 a charming red-haired young man landed with seven followers on the west coast of Scotland. He was Charles Edward Stuart 'Bonnie Prince Charlie', grandson of King James VII of Scotland and II of England. He had come to take the kingdom of Scotland from 'German George' (King George II) and make his father, James Stuart, king instead. On 19 August, supported by two of the largest Scottish Highland clans, Cameron and Clanranald, he began his attempt to reconquer Scotland and England for the Stuarts.

Charles met little opposition. On 17 September he entered Edinburgh. Four days later the English army under Sir John Cope was routed at Prestonpans, a few miles from Edinburgh. On 14 October Charles promised to undo the Act of Union of 1707 which had made England and Scotland into one country. Many Scottish people resented the union because they felt that the English had taken over their country.

Charles advanced into England as far south as Derby but there was little support from the English, and the Scots did not want to fight for the English kingdom. Charles was forced to turn back. As he marched north again many of his supporters deserted him. In April 1746 he was defeated at Culloden, near Inverness, by an English army led by the Duke of Cumberland.

Charles fled and no more attempts were made by the Stuart family to regain the thrones of England or Scotland. England and Scotland remained a united kingdom.

Most of Charles's support had come from the Highland clans, regarded by Lowland Scots as savages. The Lowlanders had benefited from the union with England. They were using new farming methods and their industries had developed trade with the whole of the British Empire. They had little enthusiasm for the Stuart cause and even less for its Highland supporters.

The failure of the 'Forty-Five' was followed by severe repression in the Highlands. The chiefs were forced into exile. The wearing of tartan and the playing of bagpipes were made illegal. Yet within forty years all this was repealed. The chiefs returned to become landowners and Highland regiments began to make their name in the British army.

Source F

Though in theory after May 1707 there was no English Parliament but wholly new 'British' legislature, in practice the English Parliament simply absorbed the Scottish one.

(J. D. Mackie, a Scottish historian, 1964)

Source G

By this great act of modern legislation, England placed on the world's highway of commerce, colonisation and culture, a small nation hitherto poor and isolated, but the best-educated and most active-minded in Europe.

(G. M. Trevelyan, an English historian, 1942)

Prince Charles Edward Stuart (Bonnie Prince Charlie)

The Highlands and Lowlands of Scotland

DIFFERENT VIEWS: WAS THE UNION A SUCCESS?

1 Charles Edward came to restore his father, James Edward Stuart, to the thrones of both Scotland and England. Why were some Scots willing to support him?

2 Did the rebellion of 1745 mean that the union of England and Scotland had failed?

3 Sources F and G describe different consequences of the union. Why do you think they have such different views?

⫶⫶⫶ Ireland

Ireland in the sixteenth century

Most Irish people belonged to the Gaelic nation. They spoke their own language and had laws and customs very different from those of the English. Although English kings had claimed to rule Ireland since the twelfth century they had controlled very little of the country. They had shown little real interest in Ireland, until the 1500s. Above is a picture of an Irish peasant.

Ulster
The most independent section of Ireland controlled by the Earls of Tyrone and Tyrconnell. The people of the eastern part of Ulster had close connections with Scotland. Families moved in both directions.

The Pale
An area controlled by the English since the 1100s. English law was used in the Pale. The Irish Parliament met in Dublin. Above is a picture of a lady from the Pale.

The Irish threat

1487 Rebellion against Henry VII launched from Ireland using Irish troops.

1493 Rebellion against Henry VII launched from Ireland using Irish troops.

1572 The Pope sent troops to Ireland as part of a plan to force England back into the Catholic Church.

1596 Spain sent troops to Ireland as part of a plan to invade England.

1641 Rebellion in Ireland led to massacre of English and Scottish settlers in Ireland.

1689 the Irish refused to accept William III and continued to support James II, helped by French troops.

1690 William victorious. Power of Protestant settlers in Ireland made certain for whole of eighteenth century.

The Elizabethan conquest – 1580s

Catholic Ireland could provide a base for Catholic countries to attack Protestant England. The English felt that they had to secure control of Ireland. English settlers were encouraged to take over land in Ireland in order to extend English control. Protestant clergy moved into Ireland. This angered the Catholic Irish and in the 1580s, led by the Earl of Tyrone in Ulster, they fought a war against the English. The Irish lost and their lands were confiscated. Under James I, English and Scottish settlers were given land, especially in Ulster, to create a population which would be loyal to the English kings and the Protestant religion.

Source H

I saw three children all eating and gnawing with their teeth the guts of their dead mother ... I saw hundreds of these poor people with their mouths all coloured green by eating nettles.

(Fynes Morrison, an English traveller who did not like the Irish)

Source I

Sir Humphrey Gilbert, one of Elizabeth's men, had the heads of all the Irish killed in one day cut off from their bodies and brought to his camp at night. The heads were laid in a line leading to his tent, so that any coming to his tent had to walk down a lane of heads. It brought great terror to the people when they saw the heads of their dead fathers, brothers, children and friends lie on the ground before them.

(Edmund Spencer, an English writer who lived in Ireland but did not like the Irish)

Rebellion – 1641

The plantation of English and Scottish settlers did not solve the problem. In October 1641 the Catholics of Ulster revolted against Protestant rule. Many of them had been deprived of their land or forced to move on to poor land. They turned against the Protestant settlers and killed four thousand of them. Others died from hunger and cold as they fled. The Ulster Catholics were joined by Catholics from the rest of Ireland. Although they wanted to make Ireland a Catholic country, their real grievance was that their lands had been given to English and Scottish settlers.

It is difficult to know what happened in the early days of the 1641 revolt. These sources will help you to understand why.

Source J

The outbreak of the rebellion in 1641 had been marked by the massacre or death by starvation of about 12,000 Scottish or English planters. This was not part of a deliberate plan. Many times Catholic priests intervened to save planters' lives.

(John Ranelagh, *A Short History of Ireland*, 1983)

Source K

In 1641 the Roman Catholic Church decided to exterminate Protestants in Ulster and there took place one of the most bloody massacres in Irish history. It was led by the priests of the Roman Catholics and the rivers of Ulster ran red with Protestant blood. The River Bann was so choked with Protestant bodies, that the Roman Catholics could walk dry shod across the river.

(Ian Paisley, September 1969)

Source L

From 22 October 1641 an attack was launched on Ulster settlers by their native neighbours, especially directed at those outside the walled towns. Possible 4,000 were killed, not counting those who died from their sufferings as refugees. Retaliatory attacks on Catholics soon accounted for nearly as many. These figures are arresting enough. But the number of victims killed in the initial 'massacre' rapidly became inflated to fantastic levels.

(R. E. Foster, *Modern Ireland: 1600–1972*, 1988)

Source M

A contemporary picture of the 'massacre' at Portadown Bridge

Driuinge Men Women & children by hund: reds vpon Briges & casting them into Riuers, who drowned not were kill'd with poles & shot with muskets.

Changes in land ownership in the seventeenth century

Areas in which land was reserved for adventurers and the army

Areas in which land was reserved for the government

Areas in which additional land was provided for the army

Areas assigned to the transplanted Catholics

Cromwell and Ireland

After the execution of King Charles I Parliament decided it had to do something about Ireland. The Members of Parliament were all Protestants who believed the massacre stories they had heard of the 1641 rebellion.

In 1649 Oliver Cromwell was sent to Ireland to re-establish English control throughout the island. Although he successfully defeated the rebels he also allowed the massacre of civilians by his troops in the towns of Drogheda and Wexford. Since that time his name has been a byword for wickedness among the Catholic Irish.

The wealthy Catholic landowners of southern Ireland had their lands taken away and were given smaller areas of poorer land in the west of Ireland. Their old land was given to English Protestants, some of them soldiers in Cromwell's army.

The type of house lived in by Irish Protestant landowners in the eighteenth century.

Source N

I had rather be overrun with a Scottish interest, than an Irish interest; and I think of all this is the most dangerous ... all the world knows their barbarism.

(Oliver Cromwell)

The Penal Laws

After Catholics supported James II at the Battle of the Boyne, special laws were passed to prevent another Catholic revival. They were known as the Penal Laws.

Source O

● No Catholic may buy land.
● On his death a Catholic's land is to be split into equal shares among his sons, **but** if one of his sons, even the youngest, becomes a Protestant, he will get **all** the land.
● No Catholic may vote in an election.
● No Catholic may be a teacher, lawyer, policeman, soldier, sailor or gamekeeper.
● No Catholic may own a horse worth more than £5.
● Catholic priests, if caught, are to be branded on the cheek with a large P.

(A summary of the Penal Laws)

Source P

Under the Penal Laws no Catholic could own a horse worth more than £5, and if a Protestant saw him with one he was allowed by law to stop him on the road, pay him £5 for it and leave him to walk.

At Mullingar [a town in the middle of Ireland], on the Dublin road, a Catholic gentleman's carriage and pair [two horses] was stopped one day by a Protestant who held £10 in his hand. The Catholic got out of his carriage, with a pistol in each hand, and shot both horses dead.

(David Thompson, *Woodbrook* (this book is an account of a Catholic family which had lost its lands)

Source Q

Never was a city better provided with learned and zealous instructors [in the Catholic religion] than Dublin is at present; we now begin to have Vespers [a Catholic service] sung and sermons preached in the afternoons. You see how peaceable times we enjoy.

(A Jesuit [Catholic] priest writing in 1747)

The Irish Protestants had all the legal rights in Ireland. They elected their own Parliament until the Irish Parliament was united with that of Great Britain in 1801. They were a small and usually rich minority who enjoyed a position of privilege unique in Britain.

1 Why did the English think they had to control Ireland?
2 **a** Why did the English try to settle Ireland with Protestants?
   b Why did the Irish rebel in 1641?
3 Ian Paisley is a leader of Northern Irish Protestants today. John Ranelagh and R. E. Foster are historians. How does this explain the differences in their accounts of the events of 1641 (Sources J, K and L)?
4 Source M is a contemporary picture of the events described by Ian Paisley.

a Do you think it was drawn by a Protestant or by a Catholic artist?
b What effect would this picture have had on the people who saw it?
Sources P and Q both describe conditions for Catholics in eighteenth-century Ireland.
a What do they tell us about how the penal laws were enforced?
b Why do they paint very different pictures of the position of Catholics in eighteenth-century Ireland?

Summary – How united was Britain in 1750?

Look back to your copy of the chart on page 57. See if you agree with the conclusions below.

England and Wales had merged into one country in the reign of Henry VIII. The same laws applied in both areas and from the point of view of government there were no differences between them. Although the richer people spoke English, many ordinary Welsh people continued to use the Welsh language and think of themselves as Welsh people.

The union with Scotland was marked by suspicion and conflict. Yet in the Lowlands (where most Scottish people lived) the people spoke English and had more in common with the English than with the people of the Highlands. The rebellion of 1745 was only supported by some Highland clans and by the 1760s many

Highlanders were joining the British army. The Scots continued to think of themselves as a separate people and kept their own laws and religion.

Ireland remained a separate country ruled by the king of England. Until 1801 it had its own Parliament. That Parliament only represented a small minority of the people of Ireland, the Protestant landowners, and its decisions had to be agreed to by the British Parliament. The majority of people in Ireland were excluded from power because they were Catholics.

In 1750 the king of England ruled other territories which were not represented in the British Parliament, such as the American colonies and Hanover in Germany. These territories did not see themselves as part of Britain.

SUMMARY: HOW UNITED WAS BRITAIN?

1 How united do you think Britain was in 1750?
2 What answer do you think the following people living in 1750 might have given to the above question:
   a an English person?
   b a Welsh person?
   c a Lowland Scot?
   d a Highlander who had supported

   the rebellion of 1745?
   e an Irish Catholic?
   f an Irish Protestant?
3 Look back to the list of reasons for change or continuity on page 8. Which causes were most important in making Britain more united? Explain your choice.

ENGLAND AT WAR

ⅮⅭ The Middle Ages

Throughout the Middle Ages English kings fought wars in Europe. When William the Conqueror became king of England he was already the ruler of Normandy in France. Owning lands in France led the English kings to quarrel with the French kings. Henry II built up the huge Angevin Empire but all the lands in France were lost in King John's reign.

Although their usual enemy was France, the English also fought in other wars. Both Richard the Lionheart and Edward I fought in the Crusades to try to recapture the Holy Land for Christians.

In the 1330s Edward III claimed to be king of France. His mother was a French princess and he was the nephew of the previous French king. The French, however, chose another king. This started the Hundred Years' War between England and France. England also had to fight the Scots who were allied with the French.

England and Europe in the Middle Ages

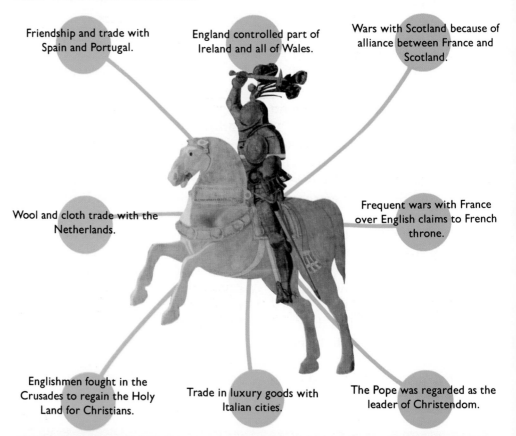

Friendship and trade with Spain and Portugal.

England controlled part of Ireland and all of Wales.

Wars with Scotland because of alliance between France and Scotland.

Wool and cloth trade with the Netherlands.

Frequent wars with France over English claims to French throne.

Englishmen fought in the Crusades to regain the Holy Land for Christians.

Trade in luxury goods with Italian cities.

The Pope was regarded as the leader of Christendom.

CAUSES AND CONSEQUENCES: ENGLAND, EUROPE AND THE WIDER WORLD

1. Why did England go to war with France and Scotland?
2. Which countries were likely to be friendly with England?
3. Which was the only area outside Europe where English people went to war in the Middle Ages?
4. English people became involved in many new areas of the world between 1500 and 1750. What were these new areas?
5. England and other European countries had little contact with other parts of the world in the Middle Ages. Why did this change?
6. Why was war in Europe more likely to spread to other parts of the world after 1500?

☿ The wider world: 1500–1750

By 1500 people had started travelling much greater distances. In 1492 Christopher Columbus, with the backing of the king and queen of Spain, set off to look for a westward route to the Far East. Instead he discovered the West Indies. In the sixteenth century the Spaniards took control of large areas of Central and South America.

In 1497 the Portuguese Vasco da Gama sailed round the southern tip of Africa into the Indian Ocean for the first time. This made it possible for Europeans to begin trading directly with the countries of the Far East for spices and other luxury goods.

Between 1519 and 1522 a Spanish expedition commanded by Ferdinand Magellan and then Sebastian del Cano sailed right round the world for the first time.

Sixteenth-century compass
Better equipment helped explorers sail in greater safety and produce better maps

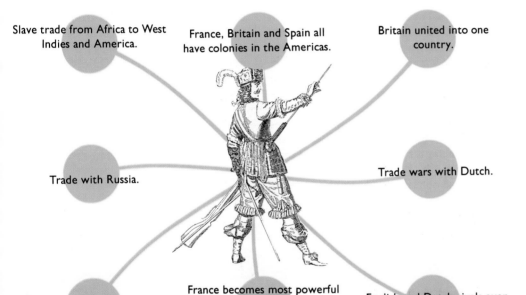

Slave trade from Africa to West Indies and America.

France, Britain and Spain all have colonies in the Americas.

Britain united into one country.

Trade with Russia.

Trade wars with Dutch.

Britain and the wider world

Pope urges Catholic countries to attack Protestant England.

France becomes most powerful country in Europe. Wars to reduce French power.

English and Dutch rivals over spice trade with Far East.

Portuguese carracks off a rocky coast, probably painted by Cornelis Antoniszoon. Ships were larger and better built so that they could sail longer distances in greater safety. Larger sails helped them to travel more swiftly.

Declaration of war
to conquer new territories from neighbours or in newly discovered lands.

Declaration of war
because the king or leader wanted to win fame and glory.

Declaration of war
to make sure other countries do not take over English trade or to take over the trade of others.

Declaration of war
to claim titles or lands which had been held by English kings in the past.

Declaration of war
to defend your religion from others or to try to impose it on other countries.

Declaration of war
to protect England from attack or to make sure that other countries do not become too powerful.

Lord Howard and Francis Drake led the English fleet which defeated the Spanish Armada in 1588. Why do you think England was at war with Spain? You can check your answer when you read page 70. This picture shows the battle.

In this chapter you will learn something about England's relations with other countries. You will be trying to answer the question:

☙ *Why did England go to war with other countries?*

Make a grid like the one below. As you work through the rest of this chapter complete the grid for each involvement or war with other countries. Use the reasons on the left to help you decide why England became involved in each war. Does Source A give you any other reasons for warfare?

Dates	Countries	Why was England involved?	Consequences

Source A

There happened to us on the 12th day of August [1568] an extreme storm which went on for 4 days, which so damaged the *Jesus* that we cut down all her higher rigging, her rudder also was sore shaken, and there were so many leaks we were forced to make for the port of St John of Ulua. [On 16 September] we saw outside the harbour 13 great ships, and understanding them to be the fleet of Spain I sent a message to the admiral telling him that I was there and that I would not let him into port unless he guaranteed our safety and promised to keep the peace. The Viceroy signed with his hand and sealed with his seal all of the conditions concluded, and forthwith a trumpet blown with command that none of either party should break the peace on pain of death. The next Thursday, being the 23 of September, at dinner time [the Spaniards] blew the trumpet and from all sides set upon us.

(John Hawkins, *The Third Voyage of John Hawkins*. John Hawkins and Francis Drake escaped from San Juan de Ulua in the only two ships that got away. Many of their fellow sailors were killed by the Spanish. Hawkins and Drake vowed vengeance on the Spanish)

England versus France – sixteenth century

Between 1511 and 1560 England was often at war with France and Scotland. As these two countries were closely allied, war with one usually meant war with the other. Henry VII had tried to ensure peace by clever diplomacy and by marrying his daughter Margaret to King James IV of Scotland. After his death his other daughter Mary married King Louis XII of France. Neither of these marriages prevented his son, Henry VIII, from going to war with both countries. The wars were very expensive and in 1558 England lost Calais, her last possession in France.

The Tudor monarchs kept up the claim to be kings of France. They showed this by including the badge of the French kings, the golden fleur-de-lys on a blue background, on their coat of arms.

Henry VIII sailing to fight the French

Source B
The king was bent on war, his (Spanish) wife and father-in-law were egging him on, the treasury was full, the country willing, the Pope calling; Henry VIII went to war against France, in search of glory and for no genuine interests of his own or his nation's.

(G. R. Elton, *England under the Tudors*, 1955)

Source C
The last years of Henry VIII were spent in war on a scale that stretched the king's resources to the very limits. Foreign policy between 1538 and 1547 cost over £2 million to finance at a time when the king's annual income was little more than £150,000.

Henry's self-imposed task was to solve the Scottish problem. He justified the war as one which was necessary to bring Scotland (in 1542) into its rightful subjection to the English throne.

(M. D. Palmer, *Henry VIII*, 1971)

Wars against France and Scotland – sixteenth century

1489 Henry VII made a treaty with Spain. A marriage was arranged between Prince Arthur and Catherine of Aragon. After 1492 Henry kept the peace with France.

1511–14 Henry VIII made war against France and Scotland in alliance with Spain and Emperor.

1522–5 War against France in alliance with Spain and Emperor.

1542 War against Scotland.

1544 War against France in alliance with Spain and Emperor (until 1546) and against Scotland (until 1551).

1557–9 War against France in alliance with Spain and Emperor.

CAUSES AND CONSEQUENCES: ENGLAND VERSUS FRANCE

1 English kings also claimed to be kings of France.
   a How did they show this claim?
   b What evidence is there that Henry VII did not take this claim very seriously?

2 What were the real reasons for war between England and France between 1485 and 1560?

3 What were the consequences for England of the wars against France and Scotland?

4 Now fill in your copy of the grid on page 68.

England versus Spain – sixteenth century

In 1588 Philip II of Spain sent the Armada to invade England and remove Elizabeth I from the throne. Although the Spaniards were defeated they still tried again twice. Thirty years earlier England and Spain had been friends and Philip had been married to Mary I. The information on this page will help you to understand why things had changed.

Scotland

Mary Queen of Scots provided a possible alternative, Catholic, ruler to Elizabeth. The Spanish encouraged English Catholics to try to murder Elizabeth and make Mary queen instead. Mary Queen of Scots was executed in 1587.

Piracy

After San Juan de Ulua English seamen like John Hawkins and Francis Drake began to attack Spanish shipping and Spanish colonies. Queen Elizabeth received some of the profits.

The Netherlands

These territories belonged to Philip II. Protestants in the Netherlands rebelled against their Catholic ruler. Elizabeth supported the rebels and, in 1585, sent an English army to help them fight the Spanish.

France

France and Spain were traditional enemies. Although the French kings were Catholics they were prepared to be friendly towards England in exchange for help against Spain.

The New World

Spain controlled much of Central and South America. She wanted to keep all the trade with this area for Spanish merchants and tried to stop the merchants of other countries. When English merchants tried to trade with Spanish colonies it sometimes led to battles like that at San Juan de Ulua in 1568.

Religion

Philip II was a devout Catholic and championed the cause of Catholics in Europe. England under Elizabeth became a Protestant country again. The English were afraid that Philip would try to force them to become Catholics.

ENGLAND VERSUS SPAIN

How would the following have explained the outbreak of war between England and Spain:
a Francis Drake?

b A sincere English Protestant?
c King Philip II of Spain?
2 Now fill in your copy of the grid on page 68.

In the reign of Elizabeth I, Protestant England's main enemy from 1585 was Catholic Spain. In the seventeenth century this changed. For most of the first half of the century England stayed out of European wars. At first the kings were too poor to make war successfully, then the Civil War took up all the attention of the English. Once the Civil War was over, the English went to war again. This time the enemy was the Dutch.

The Amboyna Massacre

The Dutch wanted to stop English merchants from trading in the East Indies for luxury goods like silks and spices. In 1623 the Dutch governor of the island of Amboyna in Indonesia arrested eighteen English merchants, tortured and executed them. James I was not prepared to go to war but it was one of the reasons why Parliament went to war with the Dutch in 1652.

Trade wars

In 1650–51 Parliament passed laws saying that foreign goods could only be brought to England in English ships or the ships of the country the goods came from. These laws were intended to take trade from the Dutch and give it to English merchants. This would have put many Dutch merchants out of business.

The English and the Dutch fought three wars between 1652 and 1674. Most of the fighting was at sea. The English won the first war. During the second war the Dutch fleet sailed up the River Medway and captured the English flagship, the *Royal Charles*. By the 1670s, however, many English people realised that Catholic France was a more serious threat to England. Although Charles II wanted to remain on good terms with the French he had to give way to the wishes of his subjects and the Dutch wars came to an end.

The Dutch attacking the English fleet in the River Medway in 1667. The English lost many ships.

John Churchill
Duke of Marlborough (1650–1722)
He rose to fame through the
friendship between his wife Sarah
and Princess, later Queen, Anne.
After the death of William III,
Churchill became commander-in-
chief of the allies fighting Louis
XIV of France and the queen's
most powerful adviser. Under his
command the allies won many
victories against the French. After
1710 he fell out of favour with the
queen and in 1712 he was
dismissed as Commander-in-chief.
He left England not to return until
after Anne's death in 1714.

The Battle of Blenheim, 1704.
Marlborough's great palace in
Oxfordshire was named after this
battle. This picture is a tapestry
from the palace.

⟩⟨ England versus France again

Since 1667 King Louis XIV of
France had been trying to make his
country more powerful by taking
over neighbouring states. In 1672
he invaded the Netherlands and
earned the undying hatred of their
ruler, William of Orange, who
became William III of England in
1688.

William and his allies won the
war in 1697. France was forced to
give up most of its conquests and
Louis XIV promised not to help
James II or his son against William.
However, peace did not last long.
All of Europe was afraid of a
French Empire dominating the
world. War began again when
Louis XIV's grandson inherited the
vast Spanish Empire. Again, the
English took part.

When William of Orange died
in 1702, an English general, the
Duke of Marlborough, took over
the leadership of the allies. He won
a spectacular series of victories
against the French: Blenheim in
1704, Ramillies in 1706, Oudenarde
in 1708 and Malplaquet in 1709.
The war eventually ended in 1713.
The union of France and Spain had
been prevented.

In the eighteenth century
Britain continued to fight in
European wars but became more
interested in her growing overseas
empire. In the second half of the
century the struggle with France
was fought mostly in India and
North America.

CAUSES AND CONSEQUENCES: THE DUTCH AND FRENCH WARS

1   Explain why the English and Dutch
    went to war:
    a from the point of view of an
    Englishman
    b from the point of view of a
    Dutchman
2   Why did the French become the main
    enemy instead of the Dutch after 1688?
3   Did England have the same reasons for
    going to war with France in the
    seventeenth century as she had in
    Henry VIII's reign?
4   Now fill in your copy of the grid on
    page 68.

During the period 1500 to 1750 bigger and better ships were built and navigation instruments were improved. These made it possible for the countries of Western Europe to reach most parts of the world.

Merchants went out to trade and colonists to settle and make new lives in far-away lands. Conflicts in such places meant that European wars began to be fought throughout the world.

In the 17th century the French set up colonies in Canada and central North America. They traded mostly in furs. They also acted as military bases from which attacks could be made on English colonies.

During the 17th century many English people went to live in North America. They established successful colonies. They produced fish, timber, tobacco and cotton.

During the 16th century English merchants began taking slaves in West Africa and selling them in North America and the West Indies. This became a highly profitable business.

In the late 17th century Britain and France began to acquire bases in India. The trade with India became very profitable and competition between the two countries was very fierce.

During the 16th century the Spanish took control of large areas of South and Central America. The gold and silver they found there made Spain rich but also attracted the attention of English pirates.

The English and Dutch East India Companies competed for the spice trade in the East Indies. Both were prepared to fight to control this profitable trade. Towards the end of the 17th century the English lost interest in the spice trade.

Between 1577 and 1580 Francis Drake led an English expedition round the world. During this journey Drake raided Spanish ports and attacked Spanish ships.

SUMMARY: ENGLAND AT WAR

On page 68 we asked why England went to war with other countries.

1 What were the most important reasons for going to war in the sixteenth century?

2 What were the most important reasons for going to war in the seventeenth and eighteenth centuries?

3 Did the reasons for going to war change? If so, why?

FINISHING YOUR INVESTIGATION

You have been investigating life in Britain between 1500 and 1750. Another way of exploring this topic is to visit one or more of the houses built at the time. Look at the pictures on these pages. What can we learn from these buildings about life between 1500 and 1750?

a

b

c

1 Put these buildings in chronological order, starting with the oldest and finishing with the one built most recently.
2 What visual clues helped you to answer question 1?
3 Match the buildings to the descriptions numbered **i** to **v**.
4 What can you learn from these buildings about whether England was becoming a more peaceful country?
5 What else can you work out from these buildings about life between 1500 and 1750?

i Herstmonceux Castle (Fifteenth century)
ii Hampton Court Palace (Early sixteenth century)
iii Burghley House (Late sixteenth century)
iv Hatfield House (Seventeenth century)
v Blenheim Palace (Eighteenth century)

d

e

Which were the most important changes?

You have seen this chart before when it was empty. By now you may have filled in the answers on your own copy of this chart. If you have, then you can compare your answers with these. You probably have more detail in the boxes than we can show here. Even if you haven't, you can still decide whether you agree with the answers in this chart.

● Which answers in column 5 do you agree with? Explain the reasons for these answers.

● Which answers in column 5 do you disagree with? Explain why you disagree.

● Do you think that Britain had become more or less united by 1750?

	1 First answer Was it an important change? (1–10)	2 Were many people affected by the changes?	3 Were the effects of the changes long-lasting?	4 Were the changes rapid or slow?	5 Revised answer Was it an important change? (1–10)	6 Did these changes help to unite Britain?	7 Do these changes still affect us today?
Religion	2	Everyone saw the changes	Yes	Rapid in the 1530's and 1550's	7	No — different religions helped to cause wars	Some people
Everyday life	6	Everyone	Yes	Sometimes quick e.g. when prices rose and there were bad harvests	10	There were still rich and poor	A little
The power of the monarch	7	Some but many could not vote	Yes	Slow until the 1680's	6	They caused wars and rebellions	Yes
England's power in Britain	4	Yes — in Ireland and Scotland	Yes	Slow	5	In some ways, in the long run	Yes
British involvement abroad	4	Yes — through trade and wars	Some of them	Empire developed slowly	7	Not very important	Only a little

How do we study history?

You have not just been learning about what happened between 1500 and 1750. You have been working like a historian – asking questions, suggesting answers or hypotheses and checking these first answers against evidence. You have also been learning more about the skills that historians need. You have been using sources as evidence. You have been investigating changes and continuities. You have been explaining the causes of events and developments.

Here are some statements that will help you to explain what you understand about the skills and ideas that historians use. Use examples from 1500–1750 to say why you agree or disagree with each statement.

CHANGE AND CONTINUITY

1 Changes in religion and politics always happened very quickly.

2 All the changes helped to improve the way people lived.

CAUSES AND EFFECTS

3 The Civil War was caused by the way Charles I governed the country.

4 A historian's task is just to list the causes and effects of an event.

PEOPLE IN THE PAST

5 Historians can study religion, politics and daily life separately because those topics did not affect each other.

6 The Scots agreed that the Act of Union would help Scotland.

7 All Charles I's opponents agreed that Charles should be executed.

DIFFERENT VIEWS

8 Which of these reasons cause historians to disagree about the past? Explain the reasons for your choice.
   a Sources are not always clear in what they say and can be interpreted in different ways.
   b Historians' own attitudes and opinions make them disagree.
   c Events and ideas at the times historians are writing make them disagree.

EVIDENCE

9 What kinds of sources tell us about Britain 1500–1750?

10 Are written sources more useful for historians than pictures?

11 What questions should you ask about a source to check whether it is reliable?

Developments in Britain: 1066–1750

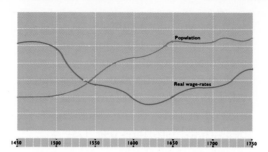

Changes in wages and the total population between 1450 and 1750

In the last two years you have studied the history of Britain since the Norman Conquest in 1066. These pages allow you to see and think about this whole stretch of history.

11th

13th

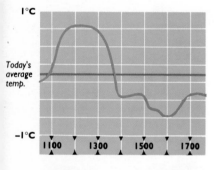

Changes in the weather between 1066 and 1750

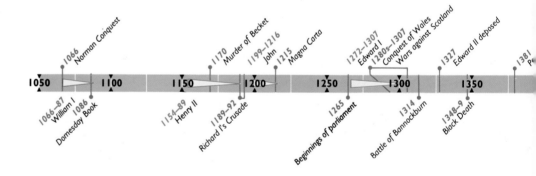

12th

14th

1 Choose the three events that you think were the most important. Explain why you chose them.
2 Choose three people who you think had the most impact on the people in Britain. Explain why you chose them.
3 Which events or developments between 1066 and 1750 still affect our lives today?
4 a In the early 1600s Francis Bacon said that three inventions changed life completely and marked the end of the Middle Ages and the beginning of modern history. They were paper and printing, gunpowder and the magnetic compass. Do you agree with him?
b Do you think that 1500 was the right date to divide up your study of British history?
5 List five things that have an important effect on your life that had not been invented by 1750.
6 If you had to live at a time before 1750, when would you choose and why?

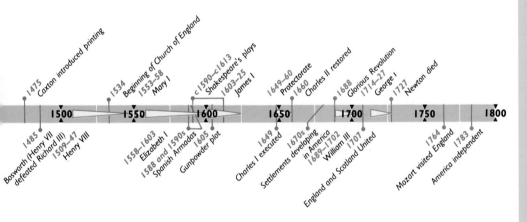

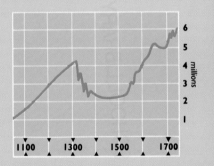

Changes in the total population from 1066–1750

INDEX

▄▄ Acknowledgements

The publishers would like to thank the following for permission to reproduce the following:

Page 31 Lambeth Palace Library, r E.T. Archive; p4tl, cl & bl National Portrait Gallery, London, tr John Blake; p5tr & cr National Portrait Gallery, br National Maritime Museum; p9 British Library 4705.h.4.1938; p10 Bridgeman Art Library/British Library; p12t & b National Portrait Gallery, c Bridgeman/Kunsthistorisches Museum, Vienna; p13t National Portrait Gallery, b Bridgeman/Wilton House; p14c & p15c National Portrait Gallery; p17tr & p18 E.T.; p19tr Fitzwilliam Museum, Cambridge, br Ashmolean Museum, Oxford; p20br Victoria & Albert Museum; p21tl & cr National Portrait Gallery, tr Royal Society; p24 Bridgeman; p25 & p26tr Bridgeman/Towneley Hall, Burnley; p26bl & p27l & r National Portrait Gallery; p28 H.M.S.O.; p29 St Bride's Printing Library; p30 British Museum; p31tr E.T., cl Hulton-Deutsch Collection; p33tc Weidenfeld & Nicolson, r National Portrait Gallery; p36t Victoria & Albert Museum, b Fotomas; p37t Mansell Collection, b British Library E 343 (ii); p38 National Galleries of Scotland/Earl of Roseberry; p39t British Museum, b Ashmolean Museum; p40t & c National Portrait Gallery; p42t Syndication International/BTA, c John Blake; p43cr British Library; p45tr Weidenfeld & Nicolson; p46tr Wellcome Institute, bc National Portrait Gallery; p47tl Bridgeman/British Library, c John Blake, br Mansell Collection; p48tr Bridgeman/Tichborne Park, Hants, tl National Portrait Gallery, cl Bridgeman/Manor House, Stanton Harcourt, Oxon, bl & br National Gallery; p49t Bridgeman, b Mansell Collection; p50t Lambeth Palace Library, b Hulton-Deutsch Collection; p51, p54tl & tc E.T.; p54tc British Library 78/72157; p55 E.T.; p58cr Bridgeman/John Bethell; p59l & r Scottish National Portrait Gallery; p61 National Portrait Gallery; p62tl & tr Biblioteek van de Rijksuniversiteit te Gent; p63 E.T.; p64 Slide File; p66 National Gallery; p67tr & bl National Maritime Museum, c Roger-Viollet; p68 National Maritime Museum; p69 Royal Collection; p71 E.T.; p72tl National Portrait Gallery, br Syndication International/Aldus Archive; p74tl & tr Michael Holford, b Syndication International/BTA; p75t Bridgeman/John Bethell, b Michael Holford.

Cover: Bridgeman Art Library   *Illustrations:* Martin Cottam   *Maps: Technical Graphics (OUP)*

ALLEYN'S SCHOOL LIBRARY